THE BOOK OF ORDINARY ORACLES

THE BOOK OF ORDINARY ORACLES

Use Pocket Change, Popsicle Sticks, a TV Remote,
THIS BOOK, and More to Predict the Future
and Answer Your Questions

Lon Milo DuQuette

WEISER BOOKS
Boston, MA/York Beach, ME

First published in 2005 by
Red Wheel/Weiser, LLC
York Beach, ME
With offices at:
368 Congress Street
Boston, MA 02210

ISBN 1-57863-316-8

2004023298

Typeset in Minion by Anne Carter
Printed in USA

This book is lovingly dedicated to Thalassa
(Queen of Air and Darkness)
and the Daughters of Divination (DOD).

CONTENTS

ACKNOWLEDGMENTS

The author would like to thank Brianna Cery for her precious tarot images, Ann Quinn for her remarkable Shakespeare Speaks oracle, Jody Breedlove for his graphics and wisdom, Kat Sanborn and Brenda Knight for their unflagging support and encouragement, and especially, the members of my Monday Night Magick Class and its most ruthless heckler, my wife Constance.

Typhon: Hast thou no message from the Gods?

Hermanubis: None, brother. Let us seek an oracle of the Gods.*

* From "The Rites of Eleusis, The Rite of Jupiter," *The Equinox*, I (6), London, Fall 1911. Reprinted by Weiser Books (York Beach, ME: 1992), Supplement, p. 24.

THiS BOOK is AN ORACLE

I cannot live without books.
—*Thomas Jefferson*

It's not too late.

IT IS said that the spoken word and the art of writing are gifts from the gods. According to tradition, the ancient Sumerians lived like the beasts of the fields until the day Oannes, the "fish man," flopped out of the Erythraean Sea and taught them letters, arts, and sciences. Thoth and Hermes did the same for the Egyptians and Greeks (only with less amphibious panache).

For centuries, writing was reserved for priests and kings. Each word or character was considered magical and holy. After all, writing mysteriously evoked pictures and ideas into the mind of the skilled reader; it allowed the dead to speak, preserved the past, itemized the present, and speculated about the future. Writing codified laws solemnized agreements and treaties, inventoried goods, tallied debts, and facilitated civilization as we know it. Is it any wonder that all writing should be held in particular reverence? Books contain astounding magical potential. Books are complex living entities and, as such, have been used for centuries as oracular devices.

For many years after the advent of the printing press, however, books remained rare, and the Holy Bible was the only book most Europeans knew or cared about. They, like many people today, considered it the "word" of God and, as such, possessed of supernatural powers. It was not uncommon for devout believers to answer their sincere questions by selecting a Bible page at random and taking from it a written answer directly from the Almighty. This process is called "bibliomancy"; used with skill and sincerity, it can be as efficacious as any form of divination.

While the Holy Bible is held in particular reverence by a great many people, others do not view it as the only holy book in the world. Indeed, as mystics of every age and culture tell us, everything is holy in its own way. Books—even ordinary ones like this one—can serve as divinatory tools.

To this end, my editor cleverly suggested that we turn this entire book into a bibliomantic oracle. I call the reader's attention to the mini oracles in the margin of this book starting on page 1. In classic oracular style, some provide direct answers, others pose provocative questions, and still others suggest that you re-ask your question and consult other oracles discussed in the book.

Just ask your question and close your eyes. Then rotate and flip the book over and over in you hands until you have no idea whether your are holding it right side up, or frontward or backward. Wait until the "spirit" moves you, then open the book to any page and read your answer. Go ahead. Give it a try. Have fun.

Oh, you are the popular one!

CHAPTER 1

NO SENSE OF HUMOR?
LEAVE MY TENT!

The human race has one really effective weapon, and that is laughter.
—*Mark Twain*

Yes, but not the way you expect.

THIS book was written to be fun. It was fun to write, and I have every confidence that it will be fun for you to read and use. Why a fun book about oracles and divination?

I guess it's because all the other books on this subject aren't very much fun, and so don't offer you the one thing that keeps us all from surrendering to the "slings and arrows of outrageous fortune" and sinking daily into cynicism, depression, hopelessness, and despair. That is the gift of laughing at it all—the gift of laughing at ourselves.

That said, please don't think that I am poking fun at the concept of oracles—even ordinary oracles. In fact, I'll bet my Magic 8-Ball that, by the time you've finished reading this little book, your soothsaying abilities will be boosted by several sooths!

Call me romantic, but I still love the word "fortuneteller." It's colorful. It cues in the soul a strum of the guitar and the lilt of a tortured violin. It evokes the smell of patchouli and garlic. It links us through racial memory to every culture's version of the goddess Fortuna—she who turns the great wheel of fortune. Sometimes we're on top of the wheel; sometimes we're not.

The image of the fortuneteller cautions us to, "Yes, take this seriously, but not so seriously that you forget that the goddess Fortuna has a sense of humor."

No sense of humor?

Zenn you offend *zee* goddess! Leave my tent!

To many of my generation (those of us who grew up in the last millennium), the word "fortuneteller" evokes images of a dark-eyed, colorfully dressed, deeply cleavaged, and heavily bejeweled Gypsy woman. She's a palm or crystal ball reader, or else she parts the veil of the unknown by reading tarot cards or any one of a number of more ordinary objects, such as playing cards, bones, dice, or dominoes.

Unfortunately, this stereotype has become synonymous with confidence scams, fraud, deceit, and larceny. Undeserved as this reputation may be in many cases, it remains an accursed legacy that casts into the twilight fringes of society both the felonious charlatan and the gifted practitioner. You only have to examine local statutes throughout the world to learn that, in many places, professional fortunetelling is a crime. For a significant part of recorded history, it was a crime punishable by death—and that's not funny at all!

So here, at the very beginning of your adventures with ordinary oracles, let's agree that, when I use the word "fortuneteller," I am referring to anyone who, by means of one or more divinatory techniques or oracles, attempts to gain knowledge of hidden things.

In the pages that follow, I share a few anecdotal examples of my attempts to gain knowledge of hidden things, and examine an assortment of common (and perhaps unlikely) divinatory tools and techniques. Some of these ordinary oracles have been used with reverence for centuries and have a rich and complex tradition. Some were created by students of my Monday Night Magick Class as part of an assignment. Some I just pulled out of my own twisted magical imagination. All of them are meant to be fun and entertaining, but they are also intended to awaken within you powers of perception that are currently slumbering just beneath your other five senses.

The subject of oracles has not always been a laughing matter. In fact, it is a very serious theme with provocative implications concerning human consciousness, the mind's potential, the fragility of time, and the nature of reality. For the greater part of recorded history, oracles have ordered wars, chosen kings and queens, and dictated the course of empires. So, before we start creating divinatory devices out of ordinary stuff we have around the house, I'm going to share with you the seven secrets every fortuneteller must know and understand.

1. You are more psychic than you think.

2. You are the oracle.

3. There is no future—only the Great Now.

Yes, but are you sure that's what you want?

4 . The oracle is the Superior Intelligence.

5 . The oracle is always right.

6 . The question is more important than the answer.

7 . Oracles work because they're perfect.

Are you ready? I have turned down the lights. I have lit the candles and incense. My eyes are closed and I am gazing into the future.

I see . . . I see . . . I see you turning the page.

No, and you'll be glad later.

CHAPTER 2

WHY ORACLES WORK—

SEVEN SECRETS OF FORTUNETELLING

It is only with the heart that one can see rightly; what is essential is invisible to the eye.
—*Antoine de Saint-Exupery*, The Little Prince

I KNOW. "Seven Secrets" sounds overly dramatic and corny. But it just so happens that six weren't enough and eight were too many. When the subject is mystical powers things just work out that way.

SECRET #1: PSYCHIC POWER? YOU'RE FULL OF IT!

Many believe that only certain people have fortunetelling "power." I personally believe that everyone is psychic—some are just more in touch with their psychic abilities than others. I haven't always felt that way. As a young occultist, I was perfectly satisfied to consider myself the most un-psychic per-

Yes, but you'll regret it.

son on Earth. A strange little episode in 1974 involving an ill-conceived practical joke forced me to rethink that attitude.

It started quite innocently, while reading tarot cards as a way of regularly earning a good meal for the three DuQuettes at the home of a wealthy acquaintance. Every Sunday, our gracious hostess threw a dinner party at her home at the marina. She invited a broad spectrum of local yogis, Rosicrucians, witches, Theosophists, spoon-benders, and various other aspiring wizards and New Age mystic poseurs. Each Sunday, after enjoying a wonderful dinner and a breath of sea air, I sang for our supper by reading the fortunes of the stuffed and wine-addled dilettantes.

I used the Crowley/Harris *Thoth Tarot* deck, which, in those days, lent me a certain air of satanic mystery. Even in those days, however, I projected such an image of banal harmlessness that nobody felt too uneasy. In fact, I think most of them secretly enjoyed their weekly brush with the "dark side."

As far as reading cards was concerned, I didn't have the slightest idea what I was doing. The cards more or less read themselves. I just laid them out on the dining room table and started talking. I certainly didn't feel that I was tapping into anything more mysterious than carbohydrates and caffeine. What little I knew about the individual cards was enough to start me blathering; then mindless free association took over.

I was amazed to see how the thoughtless bits of babbling that dropped from my lips evoked such looks of surprise and wonder from my querists. More often than not, things that made no sense to me made a lot of sense to my belching clients. At first it was fun, but after a few weeks, things took an uncomfortable turn.

Daphne was an attractive woman in her late twenties and the most devot-

Good things come in threes.

ed of the Sunday regulars. She was the kind of true believer that spiritual con-men pray for—and prey upon. She was addicted to psychic readings, and spent far too much of her time and money getting her aura fluffed and seeking astrological and psychic counseling on every aspect of her life. Our Sunday salon was just one more stop on her weekly quest for someone strange and mysterious to tell her what to think.

From the first just-for-fun tarot reading I gave her, she was totally convinced of my magical omnipotence and psychic omniscience. The more I denied it, the more she raised her eyebrows and cooed to the others in the room, "Oooo! All the *really heavy* psychics deny it."

To make matters worse, no matter how hard I tried to give her silly and stupid readings, they still turned out to be (according to Daphne) profoundly accurate. Each week, I dug myself deeper and deeper into the pit of this poor woman's delusional projections. I finally decided that, for her own good, I would do something about it.

The day before the next gathering, my wife Constance and I took a long walk and together hatched a plot—a terrible and sophomoric prank that we believed would surely bring Daphne to her senses. Our plan was this:

The next day, before the group sat down to dinner, I would take Daphne aside and tell her I had had a dream about her. Then I would tell her a story so preposterously silly that she and anyone else who might be listening would soon realize I was joking. Theoretically, after we had all shared a big laugh, I'd be able to convince Daphne that I was not the psychic guru she was looking for, and that it was very unwise for her to rely too heavily on the advice and motives of strangers.

By the time Constance and I returned from our walk, we were laughing so

You'll soon be surprised.

hard we were in tears. We concocted a story so outrageously ridiculous—so ludicrous and bizarre—we were positive it would bring Daphne back down to Earth.

That night, I rehearsed the story over and over so I could tell it with a perfectly straight face. It wouldn't be easy, and I knew timing was going to be important to pull this off. I couldn't let Daphne realize too soon that I was pulling her leg. I would need a little time to draw her deep into the phony vision before it became obvious that the whole story was an elaborate joke.

The next day, the three DuQuettes arrived at the party a few minutes late. I immediately approached Daphne (which itself was unusual, because I usually tried to avoid her).

"Daphne, could I talk to you a moment?"

Her face contorted in ecstasy as if she were having a psychic orgasm. This was going to be good.

"Yes, of course, is something wrong?"

We sat down at opposite ends of the living room couch.

"Daphne, last night I had a dream—no—it was more than a dream. Do you know what I mean? It was more like . . . more like a vision. It was about you—not *you*—Daphne—you—but *you* you. The you that once was you—and still is, obviously, but—isn't. Do you know what I mean?"

Each time I asked, "Do you know what I mean?" she wrinkled her brow knowingly, bit her lower lip, and nodded her head like a dashboard dog. I continued.

"At the beginning of the dream I felt heat on my face—a sweet heat—very, very hot. But it was a dry heat—a desert heat. Somehow I knew I was in . . . Babylon."

Daphne gasped. I had her.

"I saw a beautiful little girl—I knew it was you. Your name was Miriam, daughter of Gip."

Up to this point, everything had gone as planned, and I was having fun. But when Daphne's eyes grew as big as saucers and began to fill with tears, I realized that what I was doing was terribly wrong. What was I thinking? This was a cruel and insensitive prank. It wasn't going to be funny at all. This was a real human being I was toying with—a dear soul with feelings. I actually blushed with shame. Poor Daphne was hanging onto every word I said.

I stopped the story and looked to Constance to rescue me. She was as paralyzed as I. I searched for words of explanation—an excuse, an apology.

Daphne, of course, misinterpreted my humiliated silence as the tortured reticence of a sensitive psychic reluctant to reveal a vision of a painful past-life experience. She moved closer to me on the couch, as if to say, "Go on . . . I can take it." Other guests started to gather around us to listen. I was at a complete loss for words. The only thing I could think to do was continue the stupid story and hope for the best.

" . . . *Miriam, the daughter of Gip . . . a Hebrew slave girl in Babylon. You were only six years old when your master, a wealthy saffron broker, sold you into service to the priests of the temple of Mabooba, the great Babylonian frog goddess.*

"*Because you were born with webbed toes, you were regarded as an incarnation of the goddess. The priests doted on you and showered you with many special privileges. It was there, in the gardens of the temple complex, that you blossomed into young womanhood. You especially enjoyed buffing the giant lily pads that grew in the cool and tranquil temple ponds, and netting the sacrificial flies that fed the insatiable appetite of the great goddess.*"

It's only a game.

Daphne clumsily reached into her purse for a tissue, then wiped the mascara-stained tears from her checks. Was she hearing the same things I was saying? I felt like the most evil person on Earth. I nervously hurried the story along so I could get to the ridiculous punch line, which, by now, I was sure nobody was going to appreciate. I vowed silently I would never do anything like this to anyone ever again.

Poor Daphne was now weeping and sliding demonstrably in and out of spiritual ecstasy. I knew that, in just a few moments, when I finally sprung the trap on the poor woman, I was going to be exposed as the biggest bully in the Southern California New Age community. Finally, I neared the end of my stupid story.

"You died most horribly, when renegade priests from the Temple of Ishtar, jealous of the popularity of the frog goddess, disguised themselves as giant tadpoles and broke into the Mabooba complex, stampeding the thousands of huge and bloated votive frogs. They jammed the exits of the temple and yelled "Fire! Fire!" ... popcorn flew ... the film broke ... the projector caught fire ... the screen went blank ... and you and all the daughters of Mabooba were ... flippered to death. Every last one of you croaked."

The room fell as silent as a tomb. No one said a word.

I laughed nervously and almost shouted, "Everybody croaked!"

Silence.

Daphne stared at the floor for a moment, nodding her head slightly, as if agreeing with some internal voice. She blew her nose with a ladylike little honk, then looked at me with a fragile smile that told me she finally understood where I was coming from. I thought for a moment that maybe this hadn't been such a bad idea after all. I half expected that, at any second, she would break

You knew the job was dangerous when you took it.

into giggles of self-realization and thank me for helping her see the light. She took a deep breath and cocked her head to the side the way people do before they say something they really want you to hear.

"My name *was* Miriam."

I wasn't sure what she meant by that. The dreamy, glossy-eyed look on her face soon told me exactly what was happening.

"My name *was* Miriam. You are the third psychic to tell me this—first, a friend, then a past-life reader last week in Santa Cruz. They both saw it. I *was* born a Hebrew slave in Babylon, but I renounced my religion and became a pagan temple priestess. The other two didn't have the vision to tell me how I died. For that, I thank you. As you spoke, I could actually see myself there. I felt the heat. I smelled the pond."

I wanted to scream: "Don't you get it? What about the webbed toes? Sacrificial flies? Tadpole costumes? Bloated frog stampede? *Popcorn flying*?"

But I didn't. I just sat there and surrendered to the possibility that I might be more psychic than I thought, and that maybe, just maybe, Daphne was once Miriam, daughter of Gip, the last Priestess of Mabooba.

Of course, there is no way of proving whether or not that was a *bona fide* case of psychic ability or just another one of those synchronicities that, from time to time, make us scratch our heads and say "far out!" (Perhaps both phenomena are the same thing.) In any case, the whole episode served to change my way of looking at the mechanics of psychic abilities, and suggested to me that perhaps the key to *reading* oracles is the ability to *become* the oracle. To do that, I had to trick myself somehow into stepping out of my own way. I had to learn to train the stupid part of Lon into listening to the wise and all-knowing part of Lon. That's not always easy (the stupid part being as big as it is).

Bad things come in threes.

SECRET #2: YOU ARE THE ORACLE

To illustrate this all-important oracular secret, allow me please to share one more little story.

BookExpoAmerica is the book industry's largest annual convention held in the United States. Each year, more than 30,000 bookstore owners, publishers, distributors, authors, and celebrities gather at some big convention center and, for three days, trudge back and forth down endless aisles of booths making their annual purchases and connections.

Several years ago, to help publicize my books, my publisher asked me to appear at the company's booth and give free mini-tarot readings to anyone who wanted one (and believe me, once the sound of shuffling tarot cards poured out into the crowded aisle, everyone within earshot wanted their cards read.)

Even though these were, for the most part light, just-for-fun readings, I tried, as always, to do my best to give everyone a real reading. I was scheduled to read only from 10:00 A.M. until noon, and it was just one of those days when I was really hot with the cards. I did such a great job for the first two hours that I continued reading long past the time I was scheduled to quit. I kept right on into the afternoon, as the line of eager querists snaked past my booth. Finally, at 3:00 P.M. (and five hours of nonstop reading), I was completely drained physically, psychically, and emotionally. I was dehydrated. I had a pounding headache, and I had to . . . use the facilities. I announced that, after the next reading, I was quitting for the day.

The line broke up and everyone dispersed back into the sea of wandering souls—everyone, that is, except one smiling woman in her fifties who stood her ground and waited until I was through with my last client.

What is your purpose for visiting this dimension?

"Please," she said with the sweetest smile.

I really didn't want to disappoint her, yet I knew I wasn't going to give her a real tarot reading. For the last hour, I had just been spitting out the buzz-word meanings of the cards and actually lying when bad ones turned up. Even though I wasn't taking any money from them, I knew I was cheating these people.

"Sure," I said. "I think my kidneys are broken anyway."

The first card was The Wheel of Fortune.

Great! I thought. "Your question has something to do with a gamble or a risk of some kind."

Her face lit up and she bounced excitedly in her chair.

"Yes. My husband just bought me a bookstore. I'm here ordering my stock." I'd dodged a bullet.

The second card was The Knight of Wands.

Damn it! I hate Court cards. Even when I'm hot, I hate them. I hate them! I seldom know how to read them. Knight of Wands . . . fire of fire . . . a bearded man on a black horse. What's that? Older man? Business man? Her husband? Her father? Now what's that supposed to mean? I don't care anymore!

At any other time, the psychic juices would flow enough to give me something to say, but not any more. I just stared at the card, not knowing what to tell her. Then a tiny ember of integrity flamed up inside me.

"Tell her the truth, Lon." I told myself. "Tell her that at 10:00 A.M., you were a psychic dynamo, that you could see auras and read people's minds, that you could see the future, that you were a soothsaying, mind-blowing, prophesying, fire-breathing, New Age Isaiah . . . but no longer.

"Tell her, Lon. Tell her. If you had one scrap of integrity left in your miser-

Don't fall for flattery.

able dehydrated soul, you'd tell her you're nothing but a phony—a phony fortuneteller just shamelessly trying to get people to buy your books!"

Just as I was about to confess and throw myself on her mercy, I thought I would try to somehow lighten the moment. I picked up the Knight of Wands and, with an exasperated sigh, said, "Oh, sh**, lady! Does this have anything to do with a black horse?"

She looked at me as if she'd seen a ghost. For a second, I thought she'd been offended by my little lapse into profanity. She slapped her hand on the tabletop.

"My god! My husband just sold our racehorse to pay for the bookstore!"

I tried to appear cool, but I'm certain I looked more amazed than she.

The third card was The Fool. I silently interpreted this as a personal gaff from the gods, but I told the sweet little horseless new New Age bookstore owner that, no matter what happened with the business, she was going to have a good time with it.

In the last thirty years, I've talked to hundreds of people who consult oracles. Many are professional tarot readers. Others simply read the cards, cast the runes, or consult the I Ching (see chapter 13) for their friends and acquaintances. Almost without exception, these professional and amateur seers tell me that it is difficult, if not impossible, to get a satisfactory answer when the question concerns them.

The reason we are so good at consulting oracles for others is that, when we're detached from the question and the questioner, we become a perfect little reflection of the all-knowing (yet completely disinterested) oracular deity. When we're detached, we're free to be cavalier and indifferent—just like an oracular deity! We're free to be ruthless and rude—just like an oracular deity!

Our disinterest creates a mirror. The more disinterested we are, the clearer the mirror's surface becomes. It's easy to hold the mirror before somebody *else's* face and tell them, "Well . . . There it is! That's the way it is, you poor fool. Take it or leave it." However, the mirror of indifference becomes very cloudy when the question concerns you, and the poor fool is you.

To overcome this handicap, you must first come to the full realization that the oracle is you, and that you are a far greater intelligence than you ever imagined possible. The next thing you must understand concerns the nature of time itself.

SECRET #3: THERE IS NO FUTURE—ONLY THE GREAT NOW

Stephen Hawking said, "The laws of science do not distinguish between the forward and backward directions of time."[1] That may be easy for him to understand, but the rest of us are pretty much stuck with the illusion of time marching forward.

Since the dawn of consciousness, we've tried to look into the future to see what's coming. Personally, I don't understand why anyone would want to see the future too clearly, especially their own future. Be honest. Wouldn't it be more fun to learn unexpectedly that . . .

> Your lottery choices
>
> Will hit six out of six.
>
> You'll own two Rolls Royces.
>
> Your dividends split.

On the other hand, why would you really want to agonize in advance knowing that . . .

You're too smart for you own good.

Your lover will leave you.

Your business will fail.

Your boss will deceive you.

You'll spend time in jail.

And why would you possibly want to spoil the happy surprise of learning that . . .

Your increased libido

Will never stop slowing.

Your doctor will tell you

Your fun parts are growing.

And honestly, would it make you happy to learn that, later today . . .

That new car you cherish

Will crash with a bus

You'll hideously perish

Your face turned to mush.

The fortuneteller's third secret is that there *is* no future to look into. There is only the Great Now. The Great Now is a funny thing. Like money, it seems to be in a perpetual state of passing away. That's not really the case, however. The Great Now is in a perpetual state of *Being*. That's "Being," with a capital "B" as in "Supreme Being."

If you could actually achieve consciousness of the Great Now, you would realize and understand the wall-to-wall singularity of Being—the ecstatic consciousness of perpetual now*ness* (I know that's not a word.) You'd no longer be an observer of events and phenomena, because, in the Great Now, the observer and the observed are the same thing.

Obviously, this is a difficult concept to grasp with everyday consciousness—that part of you that thinks that yesterday somehow exists in the past and tomorrow is just the day-after-tomorrow's yesterday. You're stuck in a catch-22. In order to see the future, you must "be" in that perfect place where seeing and the seen don't exist—and neither does the future!

Confused?

That's why we have oracles.

Oracles don't show you the future or answer your questions. They are simply devices that announce the status of the Great Now. When you consult an oracle, you must somehow see the future or hear the answer to your question in that announcement. That can be very difficult . . . or as simple as opening your eyes.

SECRET #4: THE ORACLE IS A SUPERIOR INTELLIGENCE

When you consult an oracle, are you really making contact with some supernatural intelligence who actually cares at all about your health, your love-life, your lawsuits, or your publishers?

Actually . . . yes, you really are making contact with a supernatural intelligence, although supernatural may not be the best word for it. "Nature as yet unexplained" may be a better way to put it.

I could get all psychological and Jungian about this and point out that, when you successfully consult an oracle, you are really tapping into higher levels of consciousness that someday we will be able to measure with a machine and weigh on a scale, and that it is the nadir of superstition to personify and to objectify your oracular deity as our prehistoric ancestors did.

You deserve a break.

To this objection I say . . . So what?

If it works—go with it. You tap into all sorts of primal and extremely powerful cosmic and personal Ju Ju when you (even if only for a few moments) play along with the scenario . . . "With fear and trembling I approach your throne—O mighty and omniscient oracle."

Treat the oracle as a Superior Intelligence, because it *is* a Superior Intelligence. It doesn't matter if it lives in your brain, or your soul, or your liver, or your pineal gland, or in Brahma-Loka, or Valhalla, or heaven, or hell, or Graceland.

That said, it is fair to ask, "Who is this Superior Intelligence? Does it have a name? Is it a god? If so, what god?"

I can't answer those questions; at least I can't answer those questions for you. Oh, I can get on my soapbox and shout my belief that each one of us is ultimately the oracular Superior Intelligence (or, if you prefer, the microcosmic reflection of the one big Superior Intelligence). But, because you and I are different units of that inscrutable whole, we each have our own unique vocabulary of images and spiritual ideals that push the buttons of our potential oracular talents. I may prefer to imagine that I am melding with the mind of Lao Tse when I consult the I Ching. You, on the other hand, may resonate to the image of a Chinese dragon, or Buddha, or R2-D2. I've talked to one very talented tarot reader who happily considers himself an atheist and attunes himself to the residual "mental energy fields" of Albert Einstein.

In any event, you're going to have to use some technique to get out of your own way and trick your stupid self into listening to your wise and all knowing self. If you don't already have one, consider adopting a deity or some other spiritual being to personify your own personal oracular intelligence—some

Think about
how you'll be
remembered.

colorful and omniscient character you can invoke to manipulate the divination process and guide your interpretation of the answer.

It is a very common practice for tarot card and palm readers in the United States and Latin America to say a quick prayer to Jesus, the Virgin Mary, or one of the saints before proceeding. The adepts of the Golden Dawn invoked the Gnostic deity, IAO, to send Hru, the great angel they believed was especially sacred to the Hermetic forces inherent in the cards. The invocation went like this:

> I invoke thee, IAO, that thou wilt send HRU, the great Angel that is set over the operations of this secret Wisdom, to lay his hand invisibly upon these consecrated cards of art, that thereby we may obtain true knowledge of hidden things to the glory of thine ineffable Name. Amen.[2]

Whatever your feelings are about the existence or nonexistence of gods, goddesses, or spiritual entities, I'll wager you find the business of consulting an oracle more effective and accurate if you first prime the pump of your psychic potential by turning the proceedings over to a "higher power," even if you believe with your cold intellect that the higher power is ultimately you. After all, it's not your cold intellect that is doing the work or receiving the answer when you consult an oracle. So feel free to pick any character with whom you can form a devotional relationship.

Personally, I love Mark Twain, and as you will see in chapter 10, I have even developed an oracle that speaks in his words. But as deities go, I love the Hindu elephant-headed god, Ganesha. He is so cute! He is so easy for me to visualize in my mind and approach in prayer. I don't care (and neither does Ganesha) if I'm not an orthodox Hindu. When I want to come face-to-face with God, it's just easy for me to picture the face of Ganesha.

The situation is out of your control.

Use whomever or whatever you want, as long as it is an icon of your ideal of a (or *the*) higher intelligence of the universe. Invoking this Superior Intelligence is the first step toward getting out of your own way. Once you are comfortable with your relationship with the image and person of your Superior Intelligence, it will be easier for you to work with the fortuneteller's fifth great secret—"The oracle is always right."

SECRET #5: THE ORACLE IS ALWAYS RIGHT

Like it or not, you must start with the irrational supposition that the oracle actually works, and that it gives accurate answers 100 percent of the time. If you're unable to make this assumption, you may as well believe that the oracle never gives accurate answers and forget about divination altogether. If, after the fact, the oracle's answer doesn't seem to agree with your observations, you must then be willing to blame the inconsistencies upon your interpretation of the answer, and seek through analysis and meditation to resolve the seeming contradictions.

I won't lie to you. Very often, it is difficult if not impossible to get an understandable answer from an oracle. That doesn't mean, however, that you haven't received the answer. And unless you can maintain your respect for the oracle's wisdom even after it gives you an inscrutable response, you are in danger of severing your connection with the Superior Intelligence.

Put yourself in the S.I.'s place. Would you really want to continue a relationship with some moron who repeatedly pounds on your celestial door and demands that you answer his or her questions? Time and time again, you answer the door and give the poor idiot the best and most truthful answer you can; and time and time again, he or she slams the door in your face and

Who cares if it's right or wrong? It'll be an adventure.

says, "That doesn't make any sense. I guess the Superior Intelligence isn't home today."

Face it. You're the one who is not on top of the situation. Otherwise you wouldn't be turning to an oracle for answers. There is one thing that makes the interpretation process easier. In fact, it is the central secret of all divination—the question itself.

SECRET #6: THE QUESTION IS MORE IMPORTANT THAN THE ANSWER

In his book *Physics and Philosophy*, Werner Heisenberg (1901–1976), one of the greatest physicists of the 20th century and one of the founders of quantum mechanics, said, "Nature never reveals itself to us as it is, but rather always through the questions we put to it." He was obviously aware of the fortune-teller's sixth great secret.

The oracle knows everything, but for heaven's sake, don't expect it to read your mind when your mind hasn't even formulated a decent question! When it comes to consulting an oracle, you've got to do some work. You've got to be specific with your questions. If you haven't sufficiently formulated in your own mind what you want to know, then there is nothing to which the Superior Intelligence can respond.

Don't ask things like, "Should I quit my job and accept this new job offer?" You'll get an answer for sure, and the answer will be, "What kind of ridiculous question is that? What are you asking here?"

"*Should* you?" Maybe you should because it will be good for your old boss, who wishes you were gone so he could hire someone who'll work for less money?

You can't always get what you want.

"*Should* you?" Maybe you should because your new boss will now have you to replace the last poor idiot he or she drove insane?

"*Should* you?" Maybe you should because, at your new job, you will accidentally blow up the factory, killing yourself and half the town, including a little baby who was destined to grow up to be worse than Hitler and destroy the world?

"*Should* you?" How do you expect the oracle to answer that?

The oracle could answer, "For heaven's sake no! You'll kill a little baby," or "Hell yes! Go ahead. Make your enemies happy. Save the planet!"

You've got to be specific. Give your question some thought and narrow it down to what you really want answered. When you become truly serious about your question, when you discard all the stupid little questions that address only the symptoms of your predicament, when you finally come to terms with yourself as to what you really want to know, then the question *becomes* the answer. In that golden moment, the answer is everywhere, and you can see it in anything you observe.

I'm going to repeat that in bold letters:

When you actually know the question, the answer is everywhere, and you can see it in anything you observe.

And that includes the instruments of ordinary oracles.

You can see the answer by observing atmospheric phenomena, or dust clouds (aeromancy). You can see it in a rooster pecking grain (alectryomancy). You can find it in facial features (anthroposcopy), or numbers or letters or names (numerology), in the behavior of birds (augury) or the characteristics of the wind (austromancy). You can read it in random passages in books (bibliomancy), in snippets of television programs (TV roulette-o-mancy), or in water currents (bletonism) or herbs (botanomancy), or in smoke (capnomancy). You can discover it playing cards (cartomancy), or looking in a mirror (catoptromancy), or by letting molten wax drop into water (ceromancy) or examining the lines and features of a hand (chiromancy). It may come to you when you clack two rocks together (clacking) or in chance remarks or events (clidomancy), or in a crystal (crystallomancy) or finger rings (dactyliomancy). You may hear it in a person's way of laughing (geloscopy) or see it in marks on the Earth (geomancy). You may speak it after whirling around until you get so dizzy you fall down and throw up (gyromancy and vomiancy). It may appear in salt (halomancy), or in animal entrails or livers (haruspicy or hepatoscopy), in water (hydromancy) or fish (ichthyomancy), in the flame of a candle (lampadomancy) or in oil on water (leconomancy), in stones or pearls (lithomancy or margaritomancy), or in fire (pyromancy). You may discern it in moles on a body (moleosophy) or in scurrying mice (myomancy). Dead people can carry the message (necromancy), as can shadows and ghosts (sciomancy) or dreams (oneiromancy). Snakes may reveal it (ophiomancy), or the flight of birds (ornithomancy), or fountains (pegomancy), or pebbles (pessomancy). It may be hidden in the bumps on a head (phrenology) or in a face (physiognomy), in the shoulder blades of animals (scapulomancy) or in their behavior (zoomancy). It can even be found in excrement (scatoscopy) or in urine (uromancy)—yes . . . *really*!

But even though the answer can be found anywhere and in anything, it's easiest to behold it in something that is perfect.

SECRET #7: ORACLES WORK BECAUSE THEY ARE PERFECT

In *Wind, Sand, and Stars*, Antoine de Saint-Exupéry, the author of *The Little Prince*, wrote, "Perfection is achieved, not when there is nothing more to add, but when there is nothing left to take away."

The Great Now resides in perfection, and the best oracles work because they are perfect, or as closely approaching perfection as the human mind can address. Truth reveals itself in perfection. The sublime perfection of nature—the Sun, the Moon, the planets, the stars—each are characters in a cosmic spectacle acted out upon the stage of perfect universal laws. The astrologer observes these perfect movements and draws upon past indications and internal wisdom to peer into the future.

Beauty is perfection. In beauty is eternal truth revealed. The image of a dew-dappled rose can stun a sensitive heart and inspire poets to pour out their souls in verse, each line more truthful than the last. How many times have you resolved a great life question while walking on the beach or gazing at some monument of natural beauty?

Mathematics is also perfection and, even though algebra and trigonometry may have left you cold in school, the truths revealed and concealed in numbers are said to be the music of the spheres. According to the Hebrew Qabalists, numbers are the executors of creation and the key to accessing the mind of God. And as we will soon see, many of the numbers important to Qabalists are the same numbers that affect the process of divination.

In the following chapters, we'll talk specifically about some of these mathematical perfections that, when viewed with the right attitude and a mystical eye, can turn very ordinary things you have around the house into super oracles. But for the moment, let's forget about random numbers and mathematical

The way that can be told is not the constant way.

abstractions and turn our attention to another kind of perfection—the perfection that is achieved as you sink into the soft paradise of your favorite couch and stare with wagging jaw at the screen of your television while you clutch the TV remote, that wand of the oracle of the gods of the air (or the sacred cable).

Who knows does not speak.

CHAPTER 3

THE COUCH-POTATO ORACLE

There are many methods for predicting the future. For example, you can read horoscopes, tea leaves, tarot cards, or crystal balls. Collectively, these methods are known as "nutty methods." Or you can put well-researched facts into sophisticated computer models, more commonly referred to as "a complete waste of time."

—*Scott Adams*, The Dilbert Future

Wait until spring.

ANCIENT books of magick taught medieval wizards how to conjure demons and spirits to do their bidding and grant them their desires. Listed prominently among the spirits' advertised talents (which included the ability to reveal events happening hundreds of miles away) was the power to entertain the magician with all manner of poetry, music, singing, dancing, comedies, and dramas. Some of the more dangerous spirits could even show visions of naked people doing . . . well . . . things naked people do. Oh, what people did to amuse themselves before television!

Let's face it. TV is a medieval magician's dream come true—a magick mirror that informs, entertains, and (if we're not careful) enchants. Ancient wizards constantly ran the risk of the spirit gaining the upper hand and becoming master rather than slave. So it is with television. Be honest. How many hours a week does your TV vampire suck from your life? Isn't it time you took back a little of that control?

I have to confess that the idea of TV roulette-o-mancy was meant to be a just-for-fun experiment for one of our Monday Night Magick Classes on divination. It was fun, all right. But it was also surprisingly effective. Once we all got into the swing of using the remote properly, audible answers to our questions poured from the television with ruthless and hilarious clarity. If you have a television and a remote, I encourage you to try this for yourself.

When you think about it, a remote control even looks magical. It's smooth and black—covered in soft rubbery buttons labeled with numbers and geometric symbols and words like "Power" and "Mute." Some manufacturers even call it the "wand."

The Couch Potato method is very simple:

1. Make sure the remote control is programmed so that an active channel appears with every "flip" as you move either forward or backward through the channel selections. (You may, if you wish, include one blank channel to represent "no," or "nothing," or "Try again.")

2. Using the remote, mute the volume on the television.

3. Make sure you can find both the channel-select and the mute buttons with your eyes closed. Use two hands if you have to.

4. Close your eyes, ask your question aloud, and start flipping. When the spirit moves you, quickly press the mute button to activate the audio.

5. Listen carefully to the first two or three seconds of sound. Press the mute button again to turn off the sound and consider for a moment what you heard. You only want to hear the tiniest of sound bites.

6. While one word is often enough for your oracular answer, you may want to keep your eyes closed, repeat the process several times, and string together the words you hear.

The Couch-Potato Oracle, or TV roulette-o-mancy, can be downright inscrutable with its responses. Don't be too quick to dismiss the answer as invalid. Take some time to think about it. If you feel you must try it more than once, consider the subsequent answers as a continuation of the conversation. For example, my ninety-year-old mother is in failing health. This morning I asked, "What can I do to make my mother feel better?" Three consecutive answers from three different channels counseled me to

- Bring something to eat.

- Make funny faces.

- It may embarrass the child, but that's okay.

Maybe I'd better get off the couch.

Hoist it up the flagpole and see who salutes.

CHAPTER 4

THE ORACLE OF KO–WEEN

I am not bound to please thee with my answers.
—*William Shakespeare,* Merchant of Venice

Keep your cool and maintain a low profile.

IF YOU were to dig down, around, and in back of the couch pillows, I'll wager you'd find another ordinary oracle, one that is based on one of those mathematical perfections I discussed earlier. Now, I'm not talking about algebra or trigonometry. I'm talking simple numbers.

Obviously, the most profound mathematically based oracle would spring from the inscrutable number zero. Unfortunately, zero literally gives us nothing practical to work with. And the number one, which expresses its perfection in eternal monotony, isn't much better. But things get very interesting when we come to the number two (and I don't mean scatoscopy!).

Number two is the great-great-grandmother of all randomly generated figures and images. The most profoundly ordinary oracle based on the number two is something you likely have in your pocket at this very moment—the Oracle of Ko-Ween.

In order to illustrate Ko-Ween's remarkable oracular wisdom and abilities, I'll tell you another little story—one that is best told in parts.

PART I: PROLOGUE

PantheaCon is a large and very well-organized four-day annual convention of pagans, neopagans, Druids, witches, Odinites, and sundry other nature worshippers and magick users. In 2001, the lineup of speakers was impressive, and included (among myself and many others) the venerable Z Budapest, tarot immortals Brian Williams, Mary Greer, and Rachel Pollack, and modern ritualists Sam Webster and Michael and Kat Sanborn. Headlining the whole event was my personal hero, Robert Anton Wilson. There were so many stars of the subculture firmament running around the hotel that I told my audience I felt like the fourth Wise Man, whose gift was a honey-baked ham!

Shortly after I arrived, my dear friend Thalassa, tarot diva, organizer of San Francisco's annual Bay Area Tarot Symposium (BATS), and founder of *The Daughters of Divination*, cornered me to see if I would be available the next day to participate in a panel discussion about unusual divinatory techniques. She said it would be fun and relaxed. I thought for a moment and then said, "Sure."

The reason I so readily agreed to risk humiliation before a mob of knowledgeable and militant esotericists was that it just so happened that I had in my pocket (at that very moment) the most potentially powerful divinatory device in the world—an ancient and awesome prophetic tool that answers

Don't worry. Be happy.

correctly 100 percent of the time—the mother of all augury—the Oracle of Ko-Ween.

PART II: THEORY

I've heard it said that the opposite of a truth is a falsehood, but that the opposite of a Great Truth is another Great Truth. Near the top of my list of Great Truths is the one that simply states that something "either *is* or it *isn't*." Let's face it. It doesn't matter what the odds are against me winning the California lottery. If I buy a ticket, I'm either going to win or I'm going to lose.

Above the abyss that Qabalists tell us divides the actual universe from its ideal source broods an infinitely smooth environment of consciousness wherein all opposites are reconciled. There, in the transcendent playground of the Buddha and the Avatar, a thing is true only inasmuch as it contains within itself its own contradiction.

But down here in the brickyard of the phenomenal universe, things aren't so smooth. As a matter of fact, the whole shebang appears to be held together by the vibration caused by two very big bumps in the road—bumps that cause every element of mind and matter to be splashed against a canvas of polarity——on-off, light-dark, I-you, up-down, in-out, right-left, front-back, high-low, yes-no.

It's a sad commentary, but most of humanity functions as if there were only two aspects to this polarity thing—good-evil, god-devil, right-wrong, laugh-cry, sin-virtue, life-death, profit-loss, pleasure-pain, war-peace, mercy-cruelty. They ignore (or refuse to examine) the sublime secret hidden inside every hyphenated opposite—the secret of the hyphen itself. The mystery is easily revealed if we simply replace the hyphen with the words "changing to."

It's going to be OK no matter what happens.

Now we have: on changing to off; light changing to dark; up changing to down; good changing to evil; profit changing to loss; pleasure changing to pain, life changing to death, mercy changing to cruelty. This is the "change" in the Book of Changes—the I Ching (see chapter 13). This movement is the source, the wisdom, the intelligence underlying all divinatory systems, and it manifests most perfectly in the Oracle of Ko-Ween.

The ceremony for consulting the Oracle of Ko-Ween is simplicity itself. After doing whatever you need to do to put yourself in a quiet and focused state of mind, compose your question in such a way that it can be answered with a yes or a no. Then approach the throne of the Superior Intelligence of your choice, ask your question aloud, and flip a coin (Ko-Ween). You will receive an answer that is accurate 100 percent of the time. The difficulty of interpretation arises from the fact that the polaric pulse of the universe is sometimes toggled one way to make heads mean "yes" and sometimes toggled the other way to make heads mean "no." You have to figure out the direction of the toggle.

Hey . . . did I say it was going to be easy?

PART III: THE DEMONSTRATION

To demonstrate the effectiveness of the Oracle of Ko-Ween, I hoped to chronicle an actual operation or two and present the dazzling results at the next day's panel discussion. I left the festivities early and got cozy in my hotel room. For the first operation, I asked the following question:

> What words of wisdom concerning the oracle of Ko-Ween can I give to tomorrow's panel discussion on divination?

You may rightly point out that this is not a yes-or-no question. But, as you will see, the operation is a series of yes-or-no questions. (Please pay special attention to this procedure. It is also used for consulting the pendulum in chapter 12.)

The operation went like this. I showered and got into a clean sweatshirt and sweatpants (my most powerful magical vestments). To center myself and invoke divine blessing, I chanted the holy name of the elephant-headed Hindu god, Ganesha, 108 times to the tune of *Pop Goes the Weasel*. You see, I'm too lazy to memorize the entire rosary of Ganesha's 108 names, so I simply chant the name as the only word in 4 1/2 rounds of *Pop Goes the Weasel*. (For my fiftieth birthday, a dear friend gave me a Jack-in-the-Box from which a fully dressed four-armed Ganesha pops out at the appropriate moment!)

I then went into the bathroom and washed my Ko-Ween (a 1995 Denver mint quarter). I settled down on my bed and started with the preliminary determination.

I put forth the following statement: "Ko-Ween, if heads is 'yes,' make this toss heads; if tails is 'yes,' make this toss tails." I flipped and it came up heads.

I repeated my statement and flipped again. It came up heads. Heads would be "yes."

I then asked: "Ko-Ween, will you give me words of wisdom concerning the oracle of Ko-Ween that I can give to tomorrow's panel discussion on divination?" The flip came up heads—"yes."

I asked: "Are the words of wisdom to be found in a book in this room?" The flip came up tails—"no."

I was really disappointed at this, since answers from a book are usually the most effective from the Ko-Ween oracle. First you find the book, then narrow it down to a page, then a paragraph, then a sentence, then a word. I had half

Nothing you can see that isn't shown.

a dozen books with me that were now useless for this operation.

I asked: "In other written material in this room?" I flipped—tails—"no."

"On the television?" Tails—"no."

"From the radio?" Tails—"no."

"On the emergency instructions on the door?" "Anywhere in this room?"
   "Outside the window?" All tails—"no."

"In the bathroom?" Aha! Heads—"yes."

"On the left side of the bathroom?" Tails—"no."

"On the right side of the bathroom?" Heads—"yes." Getting closer.

"On the toilet end of the bathroom?" Tails—"no."

"On the end nearest the door?" Heads—"yes."

I got up and went into the bathroom. At the end of the room nearest the door were six objects: the coffee maker, four packets of coffee condiments, and a bottle of mineral water. I took everything except the coffee maker back to the bed and resumed my flipping oracle.

"Are your words of wisdom on any of these five objects?" Damn! Tails—
   "no."

"Are the words of wisdom on the coffee maker?" Bingo! Heads—"yes."

"Really? On the coffee maker?" Again, heads—"yes."

I went again into the bathroom and looked at the coffee maker. Written on top of the lid were instructions for making coffee, numbered 1 through 6. I went back to the bed.

"Are your words of wisdom among instructions 1 through 3?" Tails—
   "no."

"Are they in number 4?" " Number 5?" Both tails—"no."

"Are they in number 6? Finally! Heads—"yes."

I went into the bathroom again, this time with a pen and some hotel stationary, and wrote down the following:

> 6. Turn switch to off when carafe is empty. For safety, the unit will turn off automatically in one hour. Do not use carafe if chipped or cracked.

This wasn't going well. Granted, if I plunged deep into some meditative trance, I could probably squeeze the blood of some Zen-like profundity from the dry turnip of these words. Cue the Koto music . . .

> First, turn off switch of thy thoughts, Grasshopper. Only when carafe of mind is emptied canst thou hope to transcend two-headed dragons of polarity. But beware! Do not engage in this art if the carafe of your mind is chipped or cracked.

I could see my presentation going down in flames. These weren't the words of wisdom I had hoped for. I went back to the bed and counted the words in instruction number 6. There were twenty-seven. So I flipped 27 times." Is word number 1 a word of wisdom? Is word number 2 a word of wisdom?" . . . until I came up with the following words:

> Turn when carafe empty unit will off hour do carafe.

This made no sense at all. I'd been flipping for over an hour and I was really getting tired of the whole thing. I'd used this method dozens of times over the years and always gotten mind-blowing information. In frustration, I asked: "Are these really your words of wisdom?" Tails—"no."

Aaaaarrgh! I went back into the bathroom and looked again at the words on the coffee maker. Then it occurred to me that I had failed to include the

Show some class and let this matter drop.

number 6 that preceded the last instruction when I had calculated my other questions. I went back to the bed and flipped.

"Is 6 your message?" Heads—"yes."

I asked again: "Is 6 your message?" Heads again—"yes."

Now I had to figure out how the number 6 could be used as words of wisdom relating to this form of divination.

I asked: "Am I to counsel people to flip the coin 6 times only? Tails—"no."

Then the flim-flam man in me had an idea: "Am I to ask someone in the audience to think of a number between one and ten and if he or she says "six" it will be an impressive display of Ko-Ween's prophetic ability? Bingo! Heads—"yes."

"Really?" Again, heads—"yes."

Finally, I had my answer. I was confident that, when asked, the audience member would come up with six and that, the next day, Ko-Ween and I would be the heroes of the divinatory panel. (I asked Ko-Ween one more question before going to bed, but I'll discuss that a bit later.)

The start of the panel discussion was delayed about ten minutes to accommodate latecomers. The meeting room was packed. All the chairs were filled; every inch of floor space in front was taken by floor-sitters; many had to stand up against the walls. I hadn't expected this. There were six of us on the panel: a remarkable rune reader (whose name I regrettably forget), Eric Lewis (who divined profound answers from a book of *Calvin and Hobbs* cartoons), the angelic Brian Williams (creator of some of the most beautiful tarot cards in the world), Thena MacArthur (who divined with sheep knee bones), and the astounding Eli Sheva (a former Israeli army officer who cast lots the Old

Everything has
its price.

Testament way). I was without question the biggest putz on the panel.

I was, however, the first panelist to speak. I said I was going to make it very brief because I wanted to see Eli Sheva cast lots. I turned to Eric Lewis, the panelist seated next to me, and said, "Think of a number between 1 and 10."

"Seven," he answered.

"F*** you!" I snapped without thinking.

The audience didn't know why I suddenly blurted that out, but, for some reason, everyone thought it was really funny. I got a big laugh and a smattering of applause out of them. I was the only one in the room who knew that the rug had just been pulled out from under me and that my whole reason for being there had just been destroyed. I decided to go through with my talk and, at the end, throw myself on the mercy of the audience by saying something like, "But, as you can see, sometimes it doesn't work."

I gave them a brief introduction, then got out my notes from the night before and recounted the entire procedure. It was very funny and every time I said "yes" or "no," the audience laughed louder and louder. (The poor souls thought I was really leading up to something!) Finally, I came to the end of my story. I told them that Ko-Ween's prophecy was that I was to ask someone in the audience to think of a number between 1 and 10 and that he or she would say "6" and prove the wondrous power of Ko-Ween.

"But," I said, "as you saw yourselves, when I asked Eric here for a number, he came up with 7."

Then someone in the audience said, "But Eric's a panelist, he's not a member of the audience!"

My face lit up. "My god, you're right! Audience . . . give me a number between 1 and 10!"

Make time.

Everyone acted as if they couldn't wait to be part of the fun. "Six!" the whole room thundered.

PART IV: A QUESTION OF POLARITY

The above is a horrible example of the efficacy of the Ko-Ween oracle. If not for the goodwill of my audience, I would have been torn apart and my pieces offered up to Odin. However, the second operation I had performed the night before was surprisingly successful. I didn't bring it up during the panel discussion because, at the time, I only knew half the story. Here's what happened.

I wanted to ask a question that would demonstrate how an answer could be interpreted if the operator was unsure if heads was "yes" or "no." I decided to ask one question, but get two answers—one answer if heads was "yes," the other answer if heads was "no." Here's the question:

Tomorrow, the person sitting in the third chair from my right will be . . . ?

Table 1 shows the distribution of answers.

TABLE 1. DISTRIBUTION OF KO-WEEN ANSWERS		
PERSON	**IF HEADS IS YES**	**IF HEADS IS NO**
Man	No	Yes
Woman	Yes	No
Wearing Hat	Yes	No
Wearing a Dress	Yes	No
Color Red	Yes	No
Color Blue	No	Yes
Amused	No	Yes

Don't ask a stupid oracle!

So, according to Ko-Ween, the person sitting in the third chair to my right should be either a woman in a hat wearing a red dress (and not very amused), or a man in blue pants and no hat (but amused).

Sure enough, the next day, the person sitting in the third chair to my right (Brian Williams) was a hatless man in blue jeans who dutifully laughed at my jokes. However, because my talk about the number six (and the coffee maker and all that flipping craziness) ended in such a miraculously spectacular way, I decided the show-biz gods would be angered if I presumed to bring up anything as anticlimactic and boring as an accurate divination. I didn't even mention the second operation.

The panel discussion was my last scheduled appearance at PantheaCon. I went back to my room to lick my wounds and count my blessings. I showered, packed my bags, and checked out at the desk about an hour before I had to grab the shuttle for the airport. I checked my bag with the concierge and went into the bar for some fish and chips and a beer.

The bar was almost empty. I plopped down at a table next to the wall and watched the Lakers dribble back and forth across the screen of a silent television. The waitress delivered my beer after serving the person at the table just the other side of a support column to my right. The column prevented me from seeing the person sitting at the table, but I observed that whoever was over there was sitting three chairs to my right.

Eventually, a petite figure popped out from behind the column. She was very dark and wore a black derby hat and enormous colorful earrings. Wow! A woman in a hat three chairs to my right. She wore tight black gloves and a black trench coat I knew she would never take off to let me know if Ko-Ween was batting 1,000. No sooner had the thought crossed my mind than she

You'll never be happier than you can make yourself right now.

turned and faced me. Her hair was pulled back and stowed under her hat, and the skin of her face clung tightly to her high-cheekboned skull. Her face was expressionless as a stone. She certainly isn't amused, I thought. She took off her gloves, unzipped her travel bag, and threw them inside. Then, she unbuttoned her trench coat, took it off, folded it neatly, and laid it over the bag. She wore a perfectly tailored woman's business suit—like something Nancy Reagan would wear. It was crimson red.

PART V: EPILOGUE

As I said at the very beginning of this chapter, when you ask a question and flip a coin, you receive an answer that is accurate 100 percent of the time. The difficulty of interpretation arises from the fact that the polaric pulse of the universe is sometimes toggled one way to make heads mean "yes" and sometimes toggled the other way to make heads mean "no." The key is in the cosmic toggle switch.

The flight home was a short one. I did manage to doze off for just a few minutes before landing. I dreamed of that stupid coffee maker and the words of wisdom that I really didn't get from it. I woke up when it occurred to me that the six directions for making coffee were not the only words engraved on the machine. On the side of the device was the power switch itself and the two magical words it toggles between—the two words that perfectly reveal the very essence of KO-WEEN's great secret of polarity:

ON—OFF.

CHAPTER 5

DICE

God does not play dice.
—*Albert Einstein*

Yes he does.
—*Stephen Hawking*

The time is ripe.

SINCE an exasperated Albert Einstein made that famous statement about God not playing dice, physicists have gone back and forth about the apparent randomness of nature. For reasons that I certainly don't pretend to understand, the crux of one such debate revolves around the theoretical impossibility of measuring both the speed and the position of a particle. Einstein figured there must be some factor—some hidden variable that, once understood, would allow such measurement and thus disprove the randomness of things. As it turns out, the old boy has been proven wrong—at least about that.

Professor Stephen Hawking, in one of his surpassingly easy-to-follow public lectures, talked about the results of an experimental test that could prove or disprove hidden-variable theories.

> When the experiment was carried out carefully, the results were inconsistent with hidden variables. Thus it seems that even God is bound by the Uncertainty Principle, and cannot know both the position, and the speed, of a particle. So God does play dice with the universe. All the evidence points to him being an inveterate gambler, who throws the dice on every possible occasion.[1]

Dice are the perfect tools for generating random numbers. In later chapters of this book, I'll show you how the six-sided die, either alone or in combination with others, can be used to generate the numbers and figures for other oracles. First, however, let's look at a couple of ordinary dice oracles.

Throwing dice is perhaps the world's oldest, most popular, and universal game of chance. It is also one of the oldest and most revered divinatory methods. Dice made from ordinary things like knucklebones, bone, ivory, fruit pits, teeth, seashells, broken pottery, stones, and sticks have been found in prehistoric grave sites all over the world. Some of the earliest written records unearthed by archeologists are rules for various games and auguries that use dice.

In a very real way, the Biblical oracular practice of casting lots is a throw of the dice. (Lots were bits of broken pottery with Hebrew letters or other mystical numbers or symbols painted on them.) Many Bible scholars believe that the Urim (revelations) and Thummim (truth), those mysterious objects that were stashed in the breastplate of the High Priest of Israel and used as oracular devices to determine God's will on a particular question, were actually a form of dice.

Scripture is full of craps shooting. As Jesus hung dying on the cross, soldiers

Rephrase the question and ask again.

threw dice for his expensive seamless cloak. Book IV of the Hindu *Mahabharata* is titled "The Fatal Dice."[2] It tells how the virtuous leader Yudhishthira lost everything because he just couldn't pass up a good game of dice. The gods of Egypt loved to play dice. One of my favorite myths concerns a famous game of dice that the Moon god, Thoth (inventor of numbers and language and time), played with the other gods. This tale has many variations, so if my version is not exactly like one you've heard, I wouldn't be surprised. It goes like this.

Ra, the Sun god, liked to think that he and Nuit, the goddess of infinite space, had an exclusive relationship. She liked him well enough, but let's face it, the Sun is just one star out of many. And when you're the goddess whose body plays hostess to all the stars in the night sky . . . well let's just say she had a capacity for a whole lot of lovin'! As sure as night follows day, she became pregnant with five babies. There is much confusion in the various myths as to who the father(s) is (are), which didn't seem to concern her too much. That is, not until Ra, in a jealous rage, cursed her so that she would not be able to give birth to those babies in any day of the year. (At the time, the year was 360 days long—twelve months of thirty days.)

This was serious. Nuit was very concerned about how all this eternal swelling was going to affect her figure. She went to Thoth, one of her favorite boy toys (moonlight is so romantic), and begged him to think of some kind of loophole in the curse that could get her out of this mess. Thoth had an idea.

He challenged the rest of the gods to a grand game of dice. Either by skill, cunning, or a little cheating, Thoth eventually beat the house. As his prize, he demanded that he be allowed to add the equivalent of 1/72 of his annual moonlight to the year, thereby lengthening the calendar by five days—days that would allow Nuit to

You're not being realistic.

beat the curse and deliver her five divine babies in a new kind of year.[3]

Today, because of the popularity of role-playing games, dice come in all shapes and numbered sides. The possibilities for divining with these are mind-boggling. For our purposes, however, we are going to stick with ordinary six-sided dice with opposite faces that add to seven (1/6, 2/5, and 3/4). After all, most of you probably already have a few of these little fortunetellers lying around the house.

I have several other reasons for doing this. First, the use of the six-sided die goes back at least as far as the Etruscans (900 B.C.). These evolved from prehistoric divination with animal knuckle or knee bones, some of which can land in any one of six positions. Second, and most important, we have inherited an existing and venerable list of "throw answers," or traditional meanings attached to the different numbers. The throw answers below are my own personal lists of meanings culled from a number of classic dice divination sources and translated (as I am wont to do) into my own lazy and abbreviated language. One set consists of eleven answers (for when you use two dice), the second lists sixteen answers (for when you use three dice). The method of consulting the Dice Oracle is the same for both.

1. Throw the dice from a cup into a circular area from twelve to eighteen inches in diameter. This can be a piece of paper or cloth, or even a small hooked rug (what I use). If you are outside, you can draw a circle on the sidewalk with chalk or mark out a circle in the dirt.

2. After invoking the Superior Intelligence of your choice and concentrating on your question, take the cup of dice in your left hand (if you are right-handed) or your right hand (if you are left-handed) and shake it until the spirit moves you to toss the dice into the circle.

Out of the frying pan, into the fire.

3. If a die falls outside the circle, don't read it. If all the dice fall outside the circle, put them back in the cup and roll again. If all the dice fall outside the circle twice in a row, wait at least three hours before attempting again.

4. You can also inject an added dimension to your throw of the dice by placing a coin or other small object anywhere within the circle before you make your throw. The die that lands nearest the coin represents things, events, or people that are coming into your life. The die that lands farthest away from the coin represents things, events, or people that are moving out of your life, or will become a factor in your life far in the future.

SUPERSTITIONS SURROUNDING THE DICE ORACLE

Half the fun of getting yourself psyched up to consult an oracle is respecting the various traditions, superstitions, and taboos unique to the oracle. After all, you're already behaving irrationally or you wouldn't be consulting an oracle in the first place! Why not go ahead and play along with the mystique and romance of the process and try not to offend the powers that be?

The three big traditional taboos of dice divination are:

1. Don't consult the dice on a Wednesday.
2. Don't consult the dice on a Monday.
3. Don't consult the dice when it is hot and humid.

I have yet to discover an explanation for these simple taboos, but I have a theory or two that make sense—at least to me. They all have to do with that famous dice player of Egyptian mythology, Thoth.

The proscription against consulting the dice on Mondays and Wednesdays

If it's something only you can do, then you have to do it.

probably derives from honoring Thoth, the Moon god—also the Egyptian version of the Greek Hermes and the Roman Mercury, whose day is Wednesday. Thoth is the god who gambled his moonlight to add extra days to the calendar—days that synchronized the calendars of the Moon and the Sun. Traditionally, the Sun calendar started on July 23, when the Dog Star, Sirius, arose and signaled the inundation of the Nile and the beginning of the hot and humid days of summer that are still known to us today as "dog days."

Okay, now that you're feeling all spooky, ask your question and toss "them bones!"

TWO-DICE ANSWERS

Use the two-dice method when you have a specific question about a specific situation. Read the answers as follows:

2 . Yes!

3 . No!

4 . Danger. Be cautious with this matter.

5 . Pause and look (and think) before you leap.

6 . You will easily get your way with this situation.

7 . Your reward will depend on how much effort you put toward your goal.

8 . Be patient.

9 . Success in everything you do.

10 . Disappointment. But keep on trying.

11 . Impossible. You're asking and expecting too much (at least for the time being).

12 . This is a real long-shot. But long-shots sometimes pay off.

In three Moons, you won't even care.

THREE-DICE ANSWERS

The Tibetans use a three-dice system they call *Sho-Mo*. Use this method when you don't have a specific question, but wish to get a general forecast of events that are likely to affect you.

3 . Family problems.

4 . You really don't understand the situation. Better rethink this.

5 . A very pleasant surprise.

6 . Your luck is about to change . . . unfortunately, not for the better.

7 . You want it? You got it!

8 . Material loss.

9 . Hassles with friends, coworkers, or lovers.

10 . A happy romantic surprise.

11 . A new baby, brainchild, or the beginning of an endeavor.

12 . A sad separation. Perhaps ill health.

13 . A message of importance—good news.

14 . Something happens to bum you out.

15 . A stranger becomes a friend by helping you.

16 . Watch your step. Play with fire now and you'll definitely get burned.

17 . Something you hear causes you to modify your plans.

18 . Is everybody happy? Yes! This is the best. Happiness. Success.

Let it be.

A tarot card will answer.

CHAPTER 6

DOMINOES

Never let the future disturb you. You will meet it,
if you have to, with the same weapons of reason which today
arm you against the present.

—*Marcus Aurelius Antoninus*

Use three dice.

ITS pretty obvious that dominoes are related to (and probably descended from) dice. As a matter of fact, you can "draw" a domino by the throw of two dice. (Die or dice falling outside the throw circle count as a blank domino.)

Dominoes have been around since at least 1100 A.D. and have been wildly popular in China and other parts of Asia ever since. Chances are you have a set around the house. If not, you can buy one at any toy store or one of the larger drugstores. You only need the most common set of twenty-eight tiles.

I use a set of the heavy white plastic dominoes. Besides being much better on your karma than ivory, they have a similar feel and make a very pleasant clicking noise when you shuffle and select them.

Where dominoes are concerned, I like to keep things simple. I keep mine in a silk bag decorated with Chinese themes in gold. I shuffle them by gently kneading the bag from the outside until I feel they're ready. Then I close my eyes, speak my question aloud, and reach into the bag and remove one domino. That's my answer.

Each domino is identified first by the side with the greater number of dots, then by the side with the lesser number of dots, i.e., 6/5, not 5/6; or 3/Blank, not Blank/3.

You may wish to use a more complex spread of more than one domino to develop a story (see chapter 7). For instance, drawing three dominoes can give you a nice clean past-present-future answer. Using more than three, however, seems to muddle the answer. I've learned that, when consulting dominoes, the fewer the tiles drawn, the clearer the answer.

Today you can do no wrong.

Ouch! This is bad as it gets. This means big trouble, pain, and sorrow. Leave my tent. Don't start anything. Put the dominoes away and pretend this never happened.

A visitor—a stranger presents a business opportunity. Don't be too gullible. Keep your cool and watch your wallet (and your back).

Harmony, balance, love, happiness, victory! A most auspicious moment. Be bold and make that decision now!

Bon voyage! You're going on a trip. Keep an eye on your wallet and don't let your guard down with attractive strangers (you dog!).

Somebody's going to lose something of material value. In spite of that, old friends and get-togethers make you feel a little better.

 Success (It's about time!). For a change, you get what you want and it makes you feel great. This makes someone so jealous he or she plots to attack you. Let 'em try!

 Uh, oh! This is not so good. Problems pop up at work or with spouse or family. Jealousy (maybe even some cheating going on). Make sure you're not the one doing the cheating. Stay out of the gossip columns . . . and the saloons until this blows over.

 If this is a yes-no question, the answer is "no." Lay low, stay cool, and don't act. Surprising news of a scandal . . . maybe concerning you.

 Your money situation is going to change for the better. Luck with your love life too! Feel free to do a bit of cautious investing . . . maybe even a little gambling.

 Good luck in money matters. Bad luck in love. Jealousy and anxiety. But can you believe it? A wedding is indicated.

Your mother should know.

Trouble, misunderstanding, disappointment. You're really going to have to work hard to straighten things out. Don't dig your heels in. Forgive if you expect to be forgiven. It's a small world and life is short.

 A little bump in your financial road is coming. Get out of debt now, before the poop has a chance to really hit the fan. A marriage or partnership can bring stability and profit. Think about it.

 Reversals. Big changes—not good. Setback, deceit, theft. Be vigilant. He or she is poison. Don't touch! But wait . . . sometimes poison taken in tiny doses over a long period of time imparts immunity.

 What you thought was doomed to failure turns out to be delightfully successful. Family matters, however, may be cause for concern.

 Party! Party! Party! And you're the guest of honor! Good times and fun with friends. A trip, recreation, and relaxation.

Bad luck strikes a friend. He or she is going to need your loving consolation. Be very tactful how you handle this. As a matter of fact, this is a time to be reflective and cautious in all areas of your life.

On the rebound? You may soon be. If not in your love life, something else. Don't worry, you'll find a new distraction. You should really be worried about the financial problems that may be looming just around the corner.

Aren't you the popular one? A regular social butterfly. Out of all this fun comes something new . . . a child (or a brainchild).

Ah! A moment of peace and calm. You deserve it. Somebody may pay you a visit, drop you a line, or call with some good news or wise advice regarding your job or business.

Surprise profits! Something you already worked for pays off big-time. Cash in and leave the table. Now's not the time to let your bet ride. Don't push your luck too far with anything new and risky.

Where troops have encamped, there brambles grow.

Change is good and this means good changes. You move your home or your job, and you'll love it. Success.

Gossip, jealousy, and deceit. A friend may not really be a friend. (I hate it when that happens.) Things could get ugly. Take the high road. Don't become ugly yourself.

A friend comes to the rescue. Your big troubles will soon be over. A wedding or partnership sets you up for really *golden* golden years.

Recovery. Your luck is changing for the better. Improved relationship. This may last, but only if you stay honest and keep your nose clean.

You're going on a trip, and you're going to have a good time. Or someone else comes back from a trip and brings you something very nice. If you're in love, you'll get the guy/gal and be deliriously happy.

Here comes the judge! A lawsuit you will probably lose. So what! It's not the end of the world. You'll form a new partnership. You might even get married.

It's not a perfect circle, but it's a perfect whatever-it-is.

Things are a struggle, but they eventually go well. You need (and will receive) the kind help of friends and others. Be patient. Don't lose your temper.

Hallelujah! This is as good as it gets. This means big happiness and success. If you ever draw this one twice in a row, buy a lottery ticket, ask a movie star to marry you, demand the corner office, and order that Porsche.

Ask again in fifteen minutes.

You've got to
be joking.

CHAPTER 7

PLAYING-CARD TAROT AND THE SOLITAIRE ORACLE

*"Did the Tarot come from playing cards or
did playing cards come from the Tarot?"
"Yes."*

—*Rabbi Lamed Ben Clifford*

It's time to be
generous with yourself.

MOST of us have at least one deck of playing cards lying around the house. If you don't already own one, you can pick up a deck at any super-market, drugstore, or convenience store for about three dollars. If you can't do that, I'll show you later in this chapter how to "draw" playing cards using dice.

Playing cards are perhaps the most common oracular device in the world, and one of the gypsy fortuneteller's classic oracles of choice. They are also used in a number of other popular prophetic games, including a favorite of the DuQuette family, Gong Hee Fot Choy.[1]

To say that there are similarities between playing cards and tarot cards would be a monumental understatement. In fact, scholars continue to debate which came first. I believe both schools of thought are at least partially correct.

The standard seventy-eight-card tarot deck appears to be a combination of the cards of two games that were very popular in Northern Italy in the first half of the 15th century: *Carte da Trionfi* (Cards of the Triumph), which was eventually called *Tarocchi*, and a Turkish card game called *Mamluk*, which, according to some sources, found its way to Europe in the 1370s.

Tarocchi gave tarot the twenty-two trump cards of the Major Arcana. These cards display the characters and images most of us think of when we hear the word "tarot"—The Fool, High Priestess, Wheel of Fortune, Death, etc. (see chapter 12). The only tarot trump that remains in a deck of modern playing cards is The Fool, now known as the Joker. I'll discuss the trumps further in chapters 8 and 9.

The Mamluk cards are essentially identical to a deck of modern playing cards. According to some authorities, Mamluk gave tarot fifty-two of the fifty-six cards of its Minor Arcana (the nontrump tarot cards).

Like a deck of modern playing cards, Mamluk had:

- Four suits: Polo Sticks, Cups, Swords, and Coins. In modern playing cards, these have become Clubs, Hearts, Spades, and Diamonds.

- Three royal cards: Sultan (King), Viceroy, and Second Deputy. These incarnated in modern playing cards as King, Queen, and Jack.

- A set of ten "pip" cards (1 through 10) for each suit.

Yes.

This arrangement mirrors almost exactly the Minor Arcana of the tarot, which also has four suits (Wands, Cups, Swords, and Disks) and ten numbered pip cards for each suit. Tarot, however, has four royal (or Court) cards for each suit: King (sometimes called the Knight), Queen, Prince, and Princess (sometimes also called the Page).

In a classic tarot reading, the fifty-six cards of the Minor Arcana (the Court cards and pips) play a very important divinatory role. The forty pip cards represent the very nuts and bolts of everyday human life—love and romance, business and money, conflicts, victories, changes, success, or failure. The Court cards, while having situational meaning, can also represent real people in certain contexts. It is from these cards that you are most likely to find understandable, straightforward answers to your divinatory questions. In fact, many professional tarot readers work with spreads that employ the cards of the Minor Arcana exclusively.

The point I'm trying to drive home is that the Minor Arcana of the tarot is one of those "nearly perfect" things that I talked about in chapter 2 that can, under the right conditions, serve as a powerful oracle.

Anyone familiar with the sublime spiritual science/art known as the Qabalah can tell you precisely why these cards are so nearly perfect. The four suits represent the four divisions of existence, the Qabalistic worlds, and the four divisions of the human soul. These four divisions are further expressed by the famous Qabalistic schematic, the Tree of Life, with its ten emanations of consciousness, and . . . well . . . I think you get the picture.

You have heavy mathematical and Qabalistic perfection in your hands when you hold the cards of the tarot's Minor Arcana and, in structure at least, a deck of modern playing cards nearly approaches that perfection. Playing cards may not be as complete or as sublimely beautiful as a colorful deck of tarot cards, but, used with sincerity and skill, they are potentially the most powerful oracular instrument you have around the house.

Before we talk about the divinatory meanings of the individual cards and learn a couple of ways to read them, let's talk briefly about the general meanings of the four suits and the card that represents you, the significator.

THE FOUR SUITS

It is very easy to see the four suits of playing cards (Clubs, Hearts, Spades, and Diamonds) reflected in their tarot counterparts (Wands, Cups, Swords, and Disks or Coins). A wand is a wooden stick and so is a club. A loving cup is the romantic symbol of matters of the heart. The Italian word for sword is *spada*—spade. And the disk or coin, the symbol of material matters, finds a perfect material expression in playing cards as the suit of Diamonds.

Moreover, their general divinatory meanings are the same. Like a monarch's scepter, Clubs represent matters of control, the will, business, and constructive enterprises. Hearts represent matters of the heart, emotions, love, and romance. Spades concern the intellect and matters of the mind, and often indicate conflict, frustration, and quarreling. Diamonds concern all things material: money, property, labor, etc.

Another fundamental way of thinking about the four suits is by attributing them to the four elements of the ancients: Clubs (Wands) are fire, Hearts (Cups) are water, Spades (Swords) are air, and Diamonds (Disks) are earth.

But you don't have to delve too deeply into the mechanics that dictate the meanings of the playing cards if you don't want to, because I've thoughtfully supplied the general divinatory meanings of the cards in the pages that fol-

In your dreams.

low. Once you settle on which spread you'd like to use, you'll be ready to go.

THE SIGNIFICATOR

The significator is the card that represents you (when you read for yourself) or the querist (the person for whom you are reading). Usually the significator is the royal card that represents your birthday, or the birthday of the querist. Each of the royal cards follows the tarot tradition and "rules" a particular thirty-degree period in the year. So each one of us is represented by one of the twelve royal cards.

In addition to that, each of the pip cards (except for the four aces, which are treated differently) represents a particular ten-degree period of the year. So, in a very real sense, each of us has two birthday cards, one royal card and one pip card. (Can you see how this information might come in handy in a fortunetelling session?)

It is most common, however, to use your royal card as the significator, and to be especially aware of your pip card if it shows up in a spread. Confused? Don't be. Just find your birthday in table 2 to discover your royal- and pip-card significators (see page 66).

You may wish to write your name on the card itself so you won't forget. You can do the same with the cards that represent the birthdays of friends, relatives, or others who may have something to do with your question. As a matter of fact, to help you remember the meanings, you may wish to write any or all of the following information on the cards themselves. After working regularly with this "marked" deck, the attributes will start to sink in and you can throw it away and use a fresh deck. Splurge! They're cheap!

It's a toss up.

TABLE 2. BIRTHDAY CARDS AND SIGNIFICATORS

January 10 to February 8	**Jack of Spades**	**July 12 to August 11**	**Jack of Clubs**
Jan. 10 to Jan. 19	4 of Diamonds	July 12 to July 21	4 of Hearts
Jan. 20 to Jan. 29	5 of Spades	July 22 to Aug. 1	5 of Clubs
Jan. 30 to Feb. 8	6 of Spades	Aug. 2 to Aug. 11	6 of Clubs
February 9 to March 10	**King of Hearts**	**August 12 to September 11**	**King of Diamonds**
Feb. 9 to Feb. 18	7 of Spades	Aug. 12 to Aug. 22	7 of Clubs
Feb. 19 to Feb. 28	8 of Hearts	Aug. 23 to Sept. 1	8 of Diamonds
Mar. 1 to Mar. 10	9 of Hearts	Sept. 2 to Sept. 11	9 of Diamonds
March 11 to April 10	**Queen of Clubs**	**September 12 to October 12**	**Queen of Spades**
Mar. 11 to Mar. 20	10 of Hearts	Sept. 12 to Sept. 22	10 of Diamonds
Mar. 21 to Mar. 30	2 of Clubs	Sept. 23 to Oct. 2	2 of Spades
Mar. 31 to Apr. 10	3 of Clubs	Oct. 3 to Oct. 12	3 of Spades
April 11 to May 10	**Jack of Diamonds**	**October 13 to November 12**	**Jack of Hearts**
Apr. 11 to Apr. 20	4 of Clubs	Oct. 13 to Oct. 22	4 of Spades
Apr. 21 to Apr. 30	5 of Diamonds	Oct. 23 to Nov. 1	5 of Hearts
May 1 to May 10	6 of Diamonds	Nov. 2 to Nov. 12	6 of Hearts
May 11 to June 10	**King of Spades**	**November 13 to December 12**	**King of Clubs**
May 11 to May 20	7 of Diamonds	Nov. 13 to Nov. 22	7 of Hearts
May 21 to May 31	8 of Spades	Nov. 23 to Dec. 2	8 of Clubs
June 1 to June 10	9 of Spades	Dec. 3 to Dec. 12	9 of Clubs
June 11 to July 11	**Queen of Hearts**	**December 13 to January 9**	**Queen of Diamonds**
June 11 to June 20	10 of Spades	Dec. 13 to Dec. 21	10 Clubs
June 21 to July 1	2 of Hearts	Dec. 22 to Dec. 30	2 of Diamonds
July 2 to July 11	3 of Hearts	Dec. 31 to Jan. 9	3 of Diamonds

Here's How It Works

First, you or the person for whom you're reading must have a specific question. Remember what we learned in chapter 2: Don't get suckered in by the old "Tell me what the cards have to say about me" request. When a querist asks me something like that, I don't even shuffle the cards. I simply draw the first card off the top of the deck and lay it down. Then, no matter what card I draw, I say, "The cards tell me that there is no need to give you a card reading, because without a question there can be no answer . . . you may leave my tent."

After settling on the exact wording of the question, write it down on a piece of paper along with the date, hour, and location of the reading. Take the cards in your left hand and invoke the Superior Intelligence of your choice (I use the classic Golden Dawn invocation in chapter 2).

1. Concentrate on the question while you or the querist shuffle the cards for one or two minutes.

2. Once you're satisfied that the cards are thoroughly shuffled, set the deck facedown on the table and, with your (or the querist's) left hand, cut them into two piles. Place the bottom pile on top.

3. Flip the entire deck faceup on the table.

4. Fan the cards out from left to right in a large horseshoe. Practice doing this until you are able to create a beautiful arc of cards in one smooth and graceful movement. This can be a breathtaking and dramatic moment that announces in no uncertain terms that "the magick has begun." Play it up for all it's worth!

5. Without disturbing the order of the cards, locate the significator.

6. Being careful to keep the cards in order, scoop the significator and all

I don't know. Toss two dice.

the cards to its right into a stack. (With the cards still faceup, the significator should be the bottom card of the stack.)

7 . Still keeping the cards faceup, restack the left portion of the horseshoe, being careful to keep the cards in order. Now you should have two stacks, both facing upward. (The right stack has the significator on the bottom.)

8 . Place the left stack on top of the right stack and turn the whole deck over, facing downward. The significator should now be on the top of the deck——the first card you will turn over in the reading.

In most readings, the significator is not read as part of the oracle. It is simply used (as outlined above) to find yourself or the querist in the deck, and locate the mysterious place to cut the deck.

SPREADS

There are literally thousands of tarot spreads used by professional and amateur readers around the world. I give you only four examples here: three classic spreads and one personal innovation. This is not to suggest that there are only four ways to read the tarot cards. I encourage you to explore other spreads you may find in tarot literature and use the one you like the best. The important thing to remember is that, once you settle on a spread, you should use it exclusively in your readings.

Obviously, shuffling the cards and drawing one to get a simple, all-knowing answer is the most profoundly simple tarot spread. It is the method used by many of the most experienced and adept readers whose familiarity with the subtlety of meanings inherent in each card enables them to see complex and detailed answers in just one card. Drawing one card is also the preferred method for those trying to get a quick and dirty answer to a quick and dirty question.

You don't even need a deck of playing cards to create a tarot spread if you have dice around the house. Throw one die three times, or three dice once, to "draw" your card. Refer to table 3 to identify the card indicated by the dice.

TABLE 3. DETERMINING A CARD BY A THROW OF THE DICE				
Card	**Clubs** (Wands)	**Hearts** (Cups)	**Spades** (Swords)	**Diamonds** (Disks)
Ace	1-1-1	1-3-6	2-3-5	3-4-6
2	1-1-2	1-4-4	2-3-6	3-5-5
3	1-1-3	1-4-5	2-4-4	3-5-6
4	1-1-4	1-4-6	2-4-5	3-6-6
5	1-1-5	1-5-5	2-4-5	4-4-4
6	1-1-6	1-5-6	2-5-5	4-4-5
7	1-2-2	1-6-6	2-5-6	4-4-6
8	1-2-3	2-2-2	2-6-6	4-5-5
9	1-2-4	2-2-3	3-3-3	4-5-6
10	1-2-5	2-2-4	3-3-4	4-6-6
King	1-2-6	2-2-5	3-3-5	5-5-5
Queen	1-3-3	2-2-6	3-3-6	5-5-6
Jack (Tarot Prince)	1-3-4	2-3-3	3-4-4	5-6-6
(Tarot Princess) No playing card equivalent. Throw again.	1-3-5	2-3-4	3-4-5	6-6-6

Don't count your money during the game.

Three-Card Spread

The three-card spread is the one I prefer when reading for myself and others. After shuffling, find the significator and cut the cards as outlined above. Turn over the significator to represent yourself or the querist, then turn over the next three cards and place them before you from left to right in a horizontal row.

The meanings of each of the three positions do not necessarily need to be chiseled in stone. Table 4 gives three very simple examples of how each of the three positions may be read, depending upon the nature of the question.

TABLE 4. THREE-CARD SPREAD		
1	2	3
Past	Present	Future
Cause	Vehicle of change	Effect
Your wish	What opposes your wish	Outcome
What you think the question is	What the question really is	What the answer really is

The Celtic Cross Spread

The Celtic Cross is one of the most popular tarot spreads in the world. It provides you, the reader, with the opportunity to sketch an in-depth portrait of the question with the first six cards and then wind up with four brutally frank revelations of who you are, how your environment affects the question, your hopes and fears, and the final outcome of the matter.

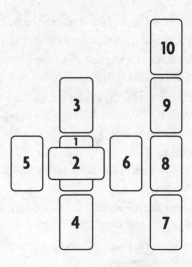

The Celtic Cross Spread

1. Shuffle and cut the cards and find the significator as outlined above.
2. Lay the significator faceup with no comment.
3. The next card in the deck will be the first card in the reading—position 1 in the figure above. Turn it over, lay it upon the significator, and say: "This card covers you and represents the general influences that surround the situation."
4. Turn over the second card and lay it across the first—position 2 in the figure—and say: "This card crosses you and shows the opposing forces, whether for good or ill."

5 . Turn over the third card and place it above the first card saying: "This crowns you and represents your conscious thought in the matter."

6 . Turn over the fourth card, place it below the first card, and say: "This card shows your unconscious thoughts in the matter."

7 . Turn over the fifth card, place it to the left of the first card, and say: "This is behind you and represents the influences that have just passed or that are now passing away."

8 . Turn over the sixth card, place it to the right of the first card, and say: "This is before you and shows the influences that will be operating in the near future."

9 . Turn over the seventh card, place it to the far right of the fourth card (see figure on page 71), and say: "This card represents yourself."

10 . Turn over the eighth card, place it directly above the seventh, and say: "This shows your environment."

11 . Turn over the ninth card, place it directly above the eighth, and say: "This card represents you hopes and wishes."

12 . Turn over the tenth and final card, place it directly above the ninth, and say: "This card tells the final outcome of the matter, the total result of all the influences exerted by the other cards."

If there is a majority of Clubs in the spread, it indicates great energy. Hearts represent emotional matters. Spades denote trouble or health matters. Diamonds point to business or financial matters. The royal cards reference social matters. More than two aces indicate great strength.

You have no say in this matter.

THE SOLITAIRE ORACLE

Do you know how to play solitaire? If you don't, I'll bet you know someone who can teach you in about two minutes. Today, most of us are introduced to the game through our home or business computers, many of which have the world's most popular version already installed.

Not everyone knows that solitaire is also a *bona fide* game of chance played in casinos. Fewer still know that it can be a powerful oracle. The most fascinating aspect of using solitaire as an oracle is that the outcome—the answer—is not just a foregone conclusion determined by cold destiny the moment the cards are shuffled and cut. By playing solitaire, you inject yourself—your decisions, your concentration, your skill, and yes, your oversights and mistakes—into the process of selecting the cards for your reading. The way you play the game is the most vital component and catalyst determining the final outcome. Kind of scary, eh?

Winning, in the old sense of the term, is not the object here. Ultimately, the answer can be a one-, two-, three-, or four-card reading that you interpret from left to right. Naturally, winning the game obviously indicates the best of fortunes, and the details of your triumphant answer are revealed, not so much by the traditional meanings of the four kings, as by your interpretation of the order of the suits. But every game is a win because the Solitaire Oracle never fails to give an answer—even if the answer is: "I have nothing to say at this time . . . try again later."

Simply ask your question and play a game of solitaire, letting the cards fall where they may. When you can go no further in the game, take note of the last cards you are able to place on top of the play stacks and then discover their meanings below.

Do it.

CLUBS

The suit of Clubs corresponds to the tarot suit of Wands and represents matters of control, the will, business, and constructive enterprises. The divinatory meanings of the cards are as follows:

King of Clubs: Action, but indicates failure if not successful on first try. If this card indicates a person, he may be a father or other married man—proud, generous, sometimes domineering.

Queen of Clubs: Constructive work under the guidance of another. If this card indicates a person, she may be a mother or other married woman—generous, attractive, with a great capacity for love, but love on her own terms. Sometimes fickle, headstrong, and brooding.

Jack of Clubs: Struggling against the odds, but winning in the very long run. If this card indicates a person, he or she may be an impetuous young person—strong and energetic. A practical joker. Can be mean-spirited and insensitive.

Ace of Clubs: The seed of action. The beginning of an undertaking. The Ace of Clubs symbolizes force—strength, energy. It implies natural rather than invoked force.

2 of Clubs: Dominion. Influence over others, authority, power.

3 of Clubs: Established strength, success. Harmony following struggle.

4 of Clubs: Perfected work. Completion. Order. Limitation. By tact and gentleness, a striven-for goal is achieved.

5 of Clubs: Strife, stress, destruction. Throwing out the old to make way for the new. Conflict. Quarreling.

It's all in your head. You just have no idea how big your head is.

6 of Clubs: Victory, accomplishment. Gain. Celebration after struggle. Harmony. Beauty. Stability.

7 of Clubs: Valor. Difficulties that require great courage and tenacity to overcome.

8 of Clubs: Swiftness. Sudden rush of energy or activity—too much, too soon. A telephone call, letter, or message. Sometimes warns of theft or robbery.

9 of Clubs: Great strength. Victory follows anxiety and fear. Strong recovery from illness. Change is stability.

10 of Clubs: Oppression. Blind force. Violent energy. Revenge. Injustice. Obstinate cruelty. Self-devouring lust after results.

HEARTS

The suit of Hearts corresponds to the tarot suit of Cups and represents matters of the heart, emotions, love, and romance. The divinatory meanings of the cards are as follows:

King of Hearts: Failure, unless extraordinary good fortune intervenes. If this card indicates a person, he may be a fair man, a bachelor perhaps, likable and honest. May be passive-aggressive in temperament, and tormented by conflicting elements of his nature.

Queen of Hearts: Beware of flattery; others see only themselves in you. If this card indicates a person, she may be an inscrutable woman, attractive and popular, completely reflective of every impression she receives.

Don't do it.

Jack of Hearts: The essentials of success are goodwill, sincerity, and right mating. If this card indicates a person, he or she may be mysterious, subtle, and intensely passionate, without conscience as ordinarily understood. He or she can be the victim of his or her own overreaching ambition.

Ace of Hearts: The seed of love. The beginning of a love relationship. The Ace of Hearts symbolizes beauty, inspiration, fertility, effectiveness, pleasure, and happiness.

2 of Hearts: Love, marriage, pleasure. Perfect harmony between lovers. Ecstasy, joy.

3 of Hearts: Abundance. Love bears fruit. Good luck and fortune. Plenty, hospitality, eating and drinking, pleasure, dancing, new clothes, merriment. Enjoy, but mistrust the good things in life.

4 of Hearts: Blended pleasure. Luxury. Unsatisfying bounty. A stationary period of happiness that may or may not continue. Success or pleasure approaching their end.

5 of Hearts: Loss of pleasure. Disappointment in love or pleasure. Expected pleasure thwarted.

6 of Hearts: Pleasure. Beginning of the fulfillment of your wish. Happiness, success, or enjoyment. Harmony. Ease. Not the gratification of superficial desires, but the fulfillment of the true sexual will. One of the best cards in the deck!

7 of Hearts: Illusory success. Debauchery. Addiction. False pleasure. Lies. Deception. Error. External splendor, internal corruption. Guilt. Fifteen minutes of drunken fame followed by a very long hangover.

8 of Hearts: Abandoned success. Indolence in success. Unpleasantness. Sorrow plagues pleasure.

9 of Hearts: Material happiness. Good fortune. Complete material success, pleasure, joy, and happiness. Wishes fulfilled.

10 of Hearts: Perfected success. Matter settled. Complete good fortune. Satiety. One's cup runneth over and stains the carpet!

Spades

The suit of Spades corresponds to the tarot suit of Swords and concerns the intellect and matters of the mind. It often indicates conflict, frustration, and quarreling. The divinatory meanings of the cards are as follows:

King of Spades: Attack. If this card indicates a person, he may be a professional—a decision-maker, active, fierce, and courageous. Can also be the victim of his own shortsightedness or ill-conceived notions.

Queen of Spades: Support comes from seemingly unsuitable sources. If this card indicates a person, she may be a confidently aggressive and keenly perceptive older woman. When she's in a good mood, she's gracious and just. But can also be cruel, deceitful, and unreliable.

Jack of Spades: Success possible, but only through the aid of an intelligence greater than your own. If this card indicates a person, It may be an ambivalent young man or woman, bright yet unfocused. A fanatic, easily attracted to fads, cults, causes, and drugs. Can be overcautious, indecisive, and unreliable.

Ace of Spades: The seed of sorrow. The beginning of an attack. The Ace of Spades symbolizes invoked force (as contrasted with natural force). The sword of justice, wrath, punishment, or affliction—for good or ill.

2 of Spades: Peace restored. Disagreement resolved, yet still some tension remains. Dormant antagonism. Pain brings forth beauty.

3 of Spades: Sorrow. Profound melancholy engendering either depression or ecstatic realization. Can mean secrecy or perversion.

Once more into the breach!

4 of Spades: Rest from strife. Tension is relaxed. Refuge from sorrow. Convalescence, recovery from illness, change for the better.

5 of Spades: Defeat, failure. Inadequate energy to maintain peace. Reason is undone by sentiment.

6 of Spades: Earned success. Intellectual endeavors rewarded. Success after anxiety and trouble. Perhaps a journey by water.

7 of Spades: Unstable effort. Futility. Indecisiveness. Yielding when victory is within grasp. Insufficient energy and will to complete the task. Perhaps a journey by land.

8 of Spades: Shortened force. Interference. Being good-natured at the wrong time. Unexpected bad luck. Energy wasted on unimportant details.

9 of Spades: Despair and cruelty. Mental anguish, illness, suffering, want, loss. Nothing moves forward. Both the acceptance of martyrdom and unrelenting revenge.

10 of Spades: Ruin, death, defeat, disruption. Undisciplined, warring force, complete disruption, and failure. Ruin of all plans and projects. So bad it makes us laugh and go on with life.

Ill met by moonlight.

Diamonds

The suit of Diamonds corresponds to the tarot suit of Disks and concerns all things material: money, property, labor, etc. The divinatory meanings of the cards are as follows:

King of Diamonds: Use your instincts. Success results from imitating nature. If this card indicates a person, he may be a sturdy man with good instincts, a business man, a breadwinner, perhaps a farmer. Unintellectual, laborious, preoccupied with material things. Can be shortsighted, stupid, and superstitious.

Queen of Diamonds: Quietly move forward. No need to battle circumstances. If this card indicates a person, she may be a quiet, practical, organized woman, affectionate, domesticated, and kind. Often shyly lustful. May attempt to seek relief from drudgery by alcohol or drugs.

Jack of Diamonds: Gradual liberation from repressive conditions. If this card indicates a person, he or she may be energetic and competent, steadfast, trustworthy; both the jack and the master of all trades. Almost emotionless, he or she may appear somewhat insensitive.

Ace of Diamonds: The seed of money. Material gain, labor, power, wealth. Materiality in all senses—good and evil—and, therefore, in a sense, illusory.

2 of Diamonds: Change—pleasant change. Visits to friends. Alternation of gain and loss, weakness and strength. Ever-changing occupation, wandering, discontent with any fixed condition. Don't worry . . . change is stability.

3 of Diamonds: Material works. Work. Constructive energy. Crystallization of forces. Job. Concentrated effort rewarded now or in the future.

I don't know.
Ask the dominoes.

4 of Diamonds: Earthly power. Gain of money or influence. A present. Mastery over purely material circumstances, luxury leading to nothing beyond.

5 of Diamonds: Material trouble. Worry. Anxiety over money. Loss of job or source of income. Prolonged inaction produces intense strain. Fundamental instability.

6 of Diamonds: Material success. Investment of labor or resources results in high yields. A settling down. Temporary success.

7 of Diamonds: Success unfulfilled. Expected profits turn into loss or even liabilities.

8 of Diamonds: Prudence, skill, or cunning. Saving for a rainy day. Plant your garden and wait. Retiring as a positive maneuver.

9 of Diamonds: Material gain. Considerable increase of fortune. Reap what you've sown and relax. Popularity. Good luck and good management. Inheritance.

10 of Diamonds: Wealth, riches. Material prosperity. Recycle wealth by acquisitions and philanthropy. If properly applied, true wisdom and perfect happiness.

Don't put it
in writing.

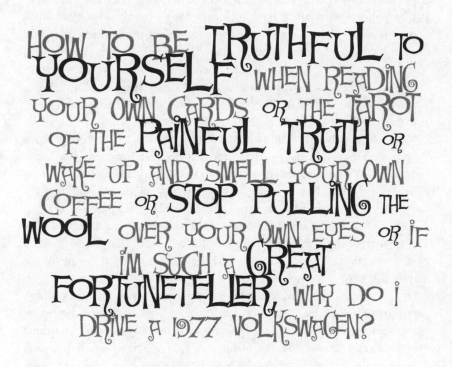

CHAPTER 8

HOW TO BE TRUTHFUL TO YOURSELF WHEN READING YOUR OWN CARDS OR THE TAROT OF THE PAINFUL TRUTH OR WAKE UP AND SMELL YOUR OWN COFFEE OR STOP PULLING THE WOOL OVER YOUR OWN EYES OR IF I'M SUCH A GREAT FORTUNETELLER, WHY DO I DRIVE A 1977 VOLKSWAGEN?

Go ahead. Make somebody's day.

This above all: to thine own self be true,
And it must follow, as the night the day,
Thou canst not then be false to any man.

—*William Shakespeare*, Hamlet

N**OW** that we've seen how to turn an ordinary deck of playing cards into the Minor Arcana of the tarot, let's see what we can do with the twenty-two cards of the Major Arcana—the cards we usually think of when we hear the word "tarot": The Fool, The Magician, The High Priestess, The Empress, The Emperor, The Hierophant, The Lovers, The Chariot, The Hermit, Strength, The Wheel of Fortune, Justice, The Hanged Man, Death, Temperance, The Devil, The Tower, The Star, The Moon, The Sun, Judgment, and The World.

Now, you may think you don't have a deck of these twenty-two tarot cards lying around the house, but you'd be wrong. You're holding one in your hands right now. The next chapter, The New Year's Eve Tarot, is illustrated by a complete set of the twenty-two tarot trumps drawn by my dear friend, Brianna Cery. They appear one to a page and you are hereby given permission make one copy of each of them to cut out and use as your personal deck of New Year's Eve tarot cards. But this chapter is not just about learning to read the twenty-two trumps. It is about how to read them for yourself . . . one of the hardest things for a fortuneteller to do.

For many years, I stopped trying to read my own tarot cards. I just couldn't detach myself from my feelings, as I can when I read for others. For many years, whenever I needed an answer to a very personal question, I consulted the I Ching (see chapter 13). The I Ching won't let me lie to myself. It doesn't care about my feelings. It even tells me when the question I ask isn't really the question I want answered. Usually, the answers are so frank, so honest, so intimate and embarrassing, that I end up wishing I had never asked the question in the first place.

What I need is an oracle that combines the cut-to-the-chase candor of the I Ching, with the convenience and the Qabalistic familiarities of tarot. I just want to shuffle my own cozy tarot deck, draw one card, and get an in-my-face I Ching-style answer? That would be so cool!

What I am about to share with you is my own personal Tarot of the Painful Truth. I don't promise that it will work perfectly for you. As a matter of fact, in order for you to be truthful to yourself, you're going to have to create your own set of divinatory answers. This is only an example of something you can create for yourself, for the times when you have a very important question and are not afraid to hear the answer.

If that moment is now, ask your question, and pick one of the cards at random from the pages of chapter 9. You can also roll a pair of dice and use table 5 to identify your card (see page 84). The most ancient existing images of the tarot card we now call The Magician show dice along with the other tools of the magician's trade—the wand, cup, sword, and disk. In fact, dice and tarot have a direct relationship with each other. Because there are twenty-one possible combinations in a throw of two dice, each throw represents one of the twenty-one numbered trump cards of the tarot. The Fool, being assigned the number zero, is "drawn" when there is any irregularity in the throw, such as one die falling off the throwing surface. Once you have determined the card indicated by your dice, find the answer to your question using the Tarot of the Painful Truth given below.

The best is yet to come.

TABLE 5. DETERMINING A TAROT TRUMP BY A THROW OF TWO DICE	
0 Fool	0
1 Magician	1-1
2 High Priestess	1-2
3 Empress	1-3
4 Emperor	1-4
5 Hierophant	1-5
6 Lovers	1-6
7 Chariot	2-2
8 Strength	2-3
9 Hermit	2-4
10 Fortune	2-5
11 Justice	2-6
12 Hanged Man	3-3
13 Death	3-4
14 Temperence	3-5
15 Devil	3-6
16 Tower	4-4
17 Star	4-5
18 Moon	4-6
19 Sun	5-5
20 Judgment	5-6
21 World	6-6

The Tarot of the Painful Truth

The Tarot of the Painful Truth is just that—painful. Some of the answers you'll read below may sound harsh, but they are intended to be so. They are intended to wake you up and shake you loose. So formulate your question carefully, draw the card or roll the dice, and, no matter what you think your question is, your answer is . . .

0. The Fool

You're being an idiot here. Forget everything you've heard about divine innocence, spiritual purity, and Parsifal. You've drawn this card because you've either done, or are about to do, the most embarrassingly stupid thing. Your friends, your enemies, your family, your coworkers, your mailman—they're all going to see what an idiot you are. The only person who is not getting the message is you! The fact that you need a tarot card to inform you of this fact is proof positive that you really *are* embarrassingly stupid. Don't try to put a good spin on this card. Don't shuffle and draw again. Don't try to read your own cards again until the situation that caused you to ask this question has resolved itself without any stupid, ill-timed, ill-conceived, ill-executed interference from you.

1. The Magician

How long do you think you can keep this up? You're not being fair to anyone . . . especially yourself. You're juggling a hundred things in the air at one time. In order to give to one, you steal from another. To be truthful to Jack, you must lie to Jill. Sure, other people may think you're really slick and creative, but deep down inside, you know you're not creating anything. You're just taking stuff that's already here and moving it around a little bit until it looks different. Big deal! To change the situation, you're first going to have to change yourself. But in order to do that, you're going to have to shut up, settle down, and focus on the real problem . . . you!

2. The High Priestess

You've forgotten something, haven't you? Something important. What is it? Funny thing about memory—if you're not careful, it will rearrange your past. It's painful to remember what a jerk you've been. It's embarrassing, like when you run across a romantic poem you wrote in high school. You just want to rip it up, burn the pieces, and bury the ashes. That's just how you'd feel if you ever allowed yourself an honest memory. What makes you think you're any less of a jerk now? Be brave. There are treasures buried in all that embarrassment . . . nuggets of who you really are . . . who you've always been. The answer to your question cannot be remembered; it must be "unforgotten." Let memories flow unhindered by judgment or editorial comment. Dive right in. Relax. Be still. Take some deep breaths. Unremembered truths float to the surface when your mind is a pool of silence. Now, what was it that you forgot?

3. The Empress

Isn't she lovely? You were glad when you drew this card, weren't you? You poor fool! I guess if your question was one of love, romance, or interior design, you should be giddy as a schoolgirl, but if it concerns real problems with real people, then you better be ready to deal with—**the prima donna!** Yep! Cherchez la prima donna. If she's another person, you'd better be ready to do some real buttering up. If the prima donna is you, you'd better check and make sure your butter is really worth "upping." In either case, somebody's going to expect the royal treatment, whether he or she deserves it or not, and you're going to have to deal with it.

Don't ignore the obvious.

4. The Emperor

Well, it looks as if you've finally forced yourself into a situation where you're in control of something. You're calling the shots now. It's only right. After all, it's your destiny, isn't it? As supreme ruler, you can now be happy and focus on building a better life, a better career, a better world—right? Yeah, just like Caesar Augustus did. Just like Tiberius, Caligula, Nero, Napoleon, and Hitler did. No doubt there have been some happy emperors. I just can't think of any. You may want to check and see if you are running the empire or the empire is running you. Good luck! Heil you!

5. The Hierophant

Hey, you're going to need some help here, and it's going to have to come from upstairs. You need advice, you need guidance, you need resources, and you need it from one or more of your superiors. Yes—I said, your superiors. Your boss, your teacher, your guru, your children, your bartender, maybe even—your spouse! Ask for help and listen hard to what they say. It's the only chance you have of ever being superior yourself!

6. The Lovers

Why were you immediately happy to get this card? Is it because you think it indicates wonderful and sexy things are about to happen to you? Is it because you think you're such a great lover that you arouse caninelike adoration from anyone you favor and suicidal heartbreak from anyone you ignore? Wake up! You've got a decision to make. Someone or something may be ready to take you on as a partner. It may be the beginning of a beautiful friendship—provided, of course, you can make up your mind. The choice should be obvious. Unless, of course, you're thinking with a part of your body other than your head.

Retreat.

I don't know. Toss three dice.

7. The Chariot

You win! The day is yours! You have overcome! You hold the prize! Your ene-mies are vanquished. You're driving a new Ferrari to your high school reunion. For a golden moment, you are secure, confident, and on your way. On your way——where? How many times in life have you dropped the ball? How many times have you had the world in your hands, but you blew it because, deep down inside, you felt you didn't deserve it. How many times have you snatched defeat from the jaws of victory? Well, in this place, at this hour, you deserve it! You deserve it as long as you truly know you deserve it. The Holy Grail is yours. Don't backwash!

8. Strength

You've got a lot of pent-up energy, don't you? That's not just energy, my friend; it's love! You've got so much love bottled up in you that you can't think. That's good. Don't think. What's thinking ever had to do with love anyway? Pop that cork and let that love gush out of you in ecstatic streams of legal and socially acceptable passion. Embrace the world with the courage and bravado of a mad gypsy dance instructor.

9. The Hermit

Put your hands behind your head, sir, and step away from the question. You have the right to—no, you *will*—remain silent. Anything you say or do will be used against you in a court of karmic law. Put yourself in protective custody, in solitary confinement. The situation will have to do without you for a while. You need to do hard time with yourself. Once you get used to being on the inside, you'll be amazed at how clearly you start seeing how things really are on the outside. Who knows, maybe someday you may become a wise guy.

10. The Wheel of Fortune

"Oh wonderful!" I hear you say. "Finally, my luck is changing!" Snap out of it! Ask yourself, how bad is your luck . . . really? Do you have clothes on your back, a warm place to sleep, food to eat, clean water to drink, friends and family members who love you? Just how much do you really want your luck to change? This card is a reminder that you live from moment to moment in the moment just before your luck is about to change. It is either telling you that things are so bad it's time for them to get better, or it's telling you that things are so good it's time for them to get worse. Which way is the wheel turning? Don't ask the cards; ask yourself.

11. Justice

You are about to get what you deserve. Go to the mirror. Look yourself square in the eyes and ask, "Am I ready to get what I deserve?" If your answer is "no," perhaps you better think in terms of a plea bargain. If your answer is "yes," you are about (to use an old dueling phrase) to "receive satisfaction."

12. The Hanged Man

Be truthful. Were you happy to see this card appear? How did you first feel when you drew it? Heartsick? Fearful? Disappointed? Apprehensive? Constrained? Restrained? Restricted? Trapped? Thwarted? Stifled? Suspended? Martyred? Good. This card is probably trying to tell you that you have every right to feel this way. You can only stay in this position for so long before all the blood runs to your head and you lose consciousness. Don't wait. Stop feeling sorry for yourself and figure out how you are going to free yourself. Start with your hands, which you mistakenly think are tied.

Either way, it
doesn't matter.

13. Death

Yes. Whatever you asked, the answer is "death." Either because of natural causes, accident, murder, or suicide, it's over, completed, accomplished, concluded, finished, executed, ended, fulfilled, deceased, terminated, discontinued, finalized, culminated, halted, extinguished, done. No use trying to stuff the soul back into the dead body of the situation. Accept the fact that it's over. If you can't do that, start searching the world for the new body in which the soul of the question has incarnated.

14. Temperance

What's going on? Suddenly your life is filled with strange bedfellows and they all make beautiful couples. Checks go with stripes, brown shoes with tuxedos, red wine with fish! Get with the program. The answer to your question lies in your ability to think outside the box, to create something new by putting something together with something else that is outrageously different. Cool down a hot thing. Heat up a cold thing. Soften up a hard thing. Harden up a soft thing. Slow down a fast thing. Speed up a slow thing. Calm down a mad thing. Stir up a complacent thing. Give a conservative a heart. Give a liberal a reality check. Give Gandhi a gun. Turn on a black light. Make a baked Alaska. Drink some fire water. Eat some sweet-and-sour. Get the picture?

15. The Devil

So what is it that you're afraid of? What have you done? You've been naughty, haven't you? None of the other cards make you feel this way, do they? Isn't it odd that the frightful image of the devil should evoke such pangs of conscience and pious soul-searching? Yes, you can be ambitious; you can be greedy; you can be lustful. But without ambition, you'll never realize your

Not left.
Not right. Straight
down the middle!

potential; without greed, you'll never acquire the energy to better yourself, your family, your community; without lust, you will never experience the ecstasy of uniting yourself with every phenomenon. Don't be such a phony. Let all that strength and creativity flow through you unencumbered by guilt and righteousness. Don't flatter yourself. You'll never be too "frightfully good" or too "perfectly evil."

16. The Tower

Your question has a boil on it. Yes, I said your question has a boil on it—a big, nasty, red, swollen, hot, throbbing, infected ugly lump that has stretched the skin of your anxiety until you just want to grit your teeth and scratch and poke and squeeze that burning unwholesome itch until it erupts with a skin-snapping pop. Blammo! Ah! Man! That really hurt! But, then, you feel so good now, don't you? The poison's been released! The pressure's off. Right now, the situation looks like a mess of blood and pus, but that's quickly cleaned up. Now the healing can begin. Enjoy the explosion. Destruction is inevitable. It's part of a cycle you wouldn't want to change even if you could. That is, unless you enjoy growing boils.

17. The Star

If you're reading these in order, I want you to read the Star last. So that's where I put it.

18. The Moon

You're creeped-out about something or you wouldn't be trying to read your own tarot cards. Now you draw one of the creepiest cards in the deck. Don't even dream about putting a good spin on this. This is the ultimate card of deception. Regardless of what you think your question was, the answer is one

Nothing ventured, nothing gained.

of the following:

Someone is lying to you.

Everybody is lying to you.

You're lying to yourself.

Someone is not as he or she appears.

Something is not as it appears.

Nobody is as they appear.

You are not as you appear.

Nothing is as it appears.

All of the above.

There is only one good thing to say about this situation.

It will pass.

19. The Sun

You conceited peacock! It's all about you, isn't it? No matter what you think your question was about, it's really all about you. Are you happy? Do people love and respect you enough? Are people saying nice things about you? Are they buying your product, your story, your BS? Did the photographer get your good side? Just remember, you're just a glowing mass of gas and dust. Sooner or later, if there's not enough of you, you'll end up a black dwarf. If there's too much of you, you'll become a black hole. Then who you gonna shine on?

20. Judgment

So it's the end of the world. Big deal. It's not really end of the world. And even if it is the end of the world, nothing lasts forever. The end of the world comes regularly. You wouldn't want to miss it, would you? It's been a good show, but it's time to pay up and call it a day. Irving Berlin hit the nail on the head, "Before the fiddler has fled, before they ask us to pay the bill, and while we still have a chance, let's face the music and dance."

21. The World

Okay! It's over. The end. Finis! You've fought the good fight. You endured to the end. The work is complete. Collect your earnings. The Mass is ended; go in peace. Elvis has left the building. If your question had anything to do with the continuation of something, forget about it and start something else. This baby's put to bed. Nighty-night.

And now I close with The Star. For those moments when I can almost touch one.

17. The Star

> Star light, Star Bright,
>
> First Star I see tonight,
>
> I wish I may, I wish I might,
>
> Have this wish I wish tonight.

For as long as I remember I've wished upon the first star I've seen in the evening sky. I even remember the very first time did it, hoisted up on my father's shoulders and giggling at the thrill of being so high off the ground. I didn't even have to think about what my wish would be.

"I want to be happy."

It was an uncharacteristically wise choice of wishes for a two-year-old, spoiled brat. Since then it's been my only first-star wish. Oh, I still have lots

Sometimes your liabilities are your best assets.

of other wishes and hopes. But when it comes right down to it, all of them don't amount to a hill of beans if I'm too unhappy to enjoy them.

So when you draw this card, think about this: Deep down inside, every man and every woman is a star. And just like your celestial brothers and sisters, you are a self-radiant and creative god. You have your own unambiguous place in the universe. Yes, it's probably good that you drew this card, because, every once in a while, whether you think you deserve it or not, you have a reason to be hopeful. You have a reason to be hopeful, because the star you must wish upon is yourself.

Ask William Shakespeare.

CHAPTER 9

NEW YEAR'S EVE TAROT

At stroke of midnight close thine eyes,
And dream and wish and fantasize,
What thou wouldst most sincerely prize
This coming year . . . Then visualize.
Now pick a card and thou shalt see
A catalyst that is the key
To things that will transformeth thee,
If thou wouldst heed its wise decree.

—*Invocation of the New Year's Eve Tarot*

It won't help to worry.

HERE'S a tarot oracle to be used on New Year's Eve, birthdays, or on the eve of any year-long endeavor. As the above poem suggests, you must have a wish or a goal in mind before you select a card. The card then delivers, not a "yes" or "no" answer, or a warning or prediction, but information about a catalyst that can transform your life in the coming year, something that can make you a person worthy of your heart's desire.

This oracle uses only the twenty-two classic tarot trump cards (plus an extra trump I have added just for fun) and the four aces. The charming designs for the cards were drawn by Brianna Cery, who has graciously agreed to allow you to make one copy of each for your own use.

Keep your mouth shut.

THE FOOL

0

THE FOOL

A pure buffoon skips toward his doom,
An abyss of profound uncertainties.
It takes a Fool to seed that womb
With all possible possibilities.

Innocence is the catalyst
The Fool's decree is clear.
By purity of heart you'll be transformed
To greet the coming year.

I

THE MAGICIAN

The Magician is a crafty boy,
He'll cause your mind to boggle.
He can't create, he can't destroy,
But boy! Can that guy juggle.

Dexterity is the catalyst.
The Magician's decree is clear.
By craft and skill you'll be transformed
To greet the coming year.

Wait until winter (or at least until things cool off).

2

THE HIGH PRIESTESS

Twixt dark and light a maid serene
Weaves spells of fascination.
Spinning moonlight veils from strands of dream
To conceal your initiation.

The female is the catalyst.
The High Priestess' decree is clear.
By virginity's power you'll be transformed
To greet the coming year.

Flip the book over
and ask again.

3

THE EMPRESS

The Empress sits before the door
Of a garden in full bloom,
At once a chaste wife and a whore,
All life within her womb.

Beauty is the catalyst.
The Empress' decree is clear.
By sweet romance you'll be transformed
To greet the coming year.

4

THE EMPEROR

A warrior king the Emperor he,
His empire firmly established.
Dictating all within his see,
His enemies killed or banished.

Domination is the catalyst.
The Emperor's decree is clear.
By ambition you will be transformed
To greet the coming year.

5

THE HIEROPHANT

A Holy Man who hears and heeds
The voice of God within him.
Sweet mystery's Priest who dares to lead
The souls of men and women.

The voice of your soul is the catalyst
The Hierophant's decree is clear.
Through inspiration you'll be transformed
To greet the coming year.

THE LOVERS

Upon the woman man looks with lust,
But the Angel is her true lover.
The man imagines what he must,
But it's a God who makes love to her.

A marriage is the catalyst
The Lover's decree is clear.
By a union you will be transformed
To greet the coming year.

The answer will come in a dream.

7

THE CHARIOT

The Holy Grail, a Victorious Knight,
Serving neither Evil nor Good,
His chariot is the mystic Shrine
Of the cup of Holy Blood.

Victory is the catalyst.
The Charioteer's decree is clear.
In triumph you will be transformed
To greet the coming year.

8

STRENGTH

To hold the lion's jaws apart
Great bravado is a must.
But stronger still than strength of heart
Is good old-fashioned lust.

Courage is the catalyst.
Strength's decree is clear.
By passion you will be transformed
To greet the coming year.

Why did you ask? You've made up your mind!

THE HERMIT

The Hermit shuns the world of wealth
On mountaintop he stands.
He hides himself within himself
But gives his light to Man.

Solitude is the catalyst.
The Hermit's decree is clear.
In silence you will be transformed
To greet the coming year.

10

THE WHEEL OF FORTUNE

Upon the rim fight creatures three
And fortune's wheel keeps spinning.
Feeling, Thought, and Ecstasy
Eternal loss and winning.

Amusement is the catalyst.
Fortune's decree is clear.
By having fun you'll be transformed
To greet the coming year.

The end is near.

II

JUSTICE

Goddess Justice sits with poise
And wields the scales and sword.
Avoid extremes; don't rock the boat
Balance is its own reward.

Equilibrium's the catalyst
Justice's decree is clear.
At gravity's point you'll be transformed
To greet the coming year.

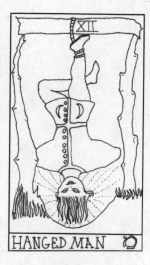

12

THE HANGED MAN

A martyred man suspended tight,
Crucified or drowned.
Truth mirrors Truth; Light mirrors Light
Even when you're upside down.

Reversal is the catalyst.
The Hanged Man's decree is clear.
Through sacrifice you'll be transformed
To greet the coming year.

He loves you.

13

DƎﱭTH

Sometimes the Death card really means death,
Sometimes . . . but very seldom.
It brings the end of unbearable stress
When any change is welcome.

A grand finale is the catalyst.
Death's decree is clear.
Through inevitable change you'll be transformed
To greet the coming year.

14

TEMPERANCE

The Angel Temperance evokes a mist
Of steam from magick born,
Of water and fire most subtly mixed
With light the rainbow forms.

Union of opposites is the catalyst.
Temperance's decree is clear.
By alchemy you'll be transformed
To greet the coming year.

Don't be too
proud to ask for directions.

15

THE DEVIL

Bad sees bad; good sees good.
Ignorance is the greatest evil.
The ignorant just look at God
And see nothing but the Devil.

Temptation is the catalyst.
The Devil's decree is clear.
Transmute a vice—you'll be transformed
To greet the coming year.

16

THE TOWER

The House of God, a Tower high
By God's own hand is blasted.
But the world would stop; all life would die
If forever had it lasted.

Destruction is the catalyst.
The Tower's decree is clear.
By war and danger you'll be transformed
To greet the coming year.

17

THE STAR

Every man and woman is a star
Most glorious and resplendent.
Would each of us know who we are
Self-radiant and independent.

Hope is the catalyst.
The Star's decree is clear.
By your inner light you'll be transformed
To greet the coming year.

18

THE MOON

She's constant inconstancy,
Her glamour ever changing.
The Moon's allure is never sure,
Eternally waxing and waning.

Illusion is the catalyst.
The Moon's decree is clear.
By seeing through it you'll be transformed
To greet the coming year.

THE SUN

Lord of all terrestrial life
Your rays we daily cherish.
Source of liberty, source of light
Without whom all would perish.

Self-image is the catalyst.
The Sun's decree is clear.
By shamelessness you'll be transformed
To greet the coming year.

I don't know. Consult the I Ching of Mi-Lo.

20

JUDGEMENT

Apocalypse comes regularly.
We may as well learn to face it.
The world breaks down periodically.
It's just easier to replace it.

Resolution is the catalyst.
Judgment decree is clear.
Make a decision and you'll be transformed
To greet the coming year.

21

THE WORLD

Amid the stars a dancer whirls
To the music of creation.
Each turn transforms a World fulfilled,
Into a World of expectation.

Patience is the catalyst.
The World's decree is clear.
With year and time you'll be transformed
To greet the coming year.

Draw your own face here.

22

THE SCREW-UP

The Screw-up stands where he shouldn't stand,
Says things he shouldn't say.
Lets opportunities slip through his hands,
And screws up every day.

Incompetence is the catalyst.
The Screw-up's decree is clear.
By blundering you'll be transformed
To greet the coming year.

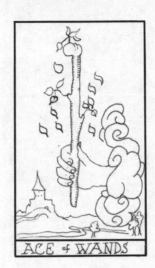

ᴀᴄᴇ ᴏf Wᴀɴᴅꜱ

The Ace of Wands, the Soul's True Will,
The purpose for your existence.
Discover your Will and you shall kill
The source of all resistance.

Your True Will is the catalyst.
Ace of Wands' decree is clear.
By self-control you'll be transformed
To greet the coming year.

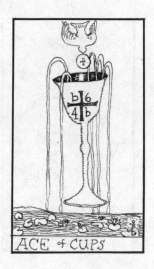

Ace of Cups

The Ace of Cups is love for sure.
Perhaps a wound from Cupid,
Or Platonic love that's far more pure,
But you'll still act just as stupid.

Love is the catalyst.
Ace of Cups' decree is clear.
With loving heart you'll be transformed
To greet the coming year.

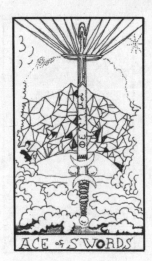

That's not your
real question.

ACE OF SWORDS

The Ace of Swords is power invoked,
Authority and discrimination.
A deadly tool when you're provoked,
Dread source of consternation.

Contention is the catalyst.
Ace of Swords' decree is clear.
Through altercation you'll be transformed
To greet the coming year.

ACE of DISKS

Ace of Disks

Ace of Disks, the Physical Plane,
It's what you think is real.
It's real like rocks; it's real like pain,
What you see, hear, taste, and feel.

Property is the catalyst.
Ace of Disks' decree is clear.
By money you will be transformed
To greet the coming year.

CHAPTER 10

THE MARK TWAIN ORACLE

Devil follow corpse, cat follow devil,
warts follow cat, I'm done with ye!

Huckleberry Finn in Tom Sawyer—*Mark Twain*

What are
you hiding?

SINCE January 1978, our Monday Night Magick Class has been peopled with a colorful mixture of seasoned adepts, eager neophytes, and everything in between. I'm not being modest when I say that they have taught me more about magick than I could ever teach them. This has always been a free event (although a donation basket is conspicuously placed near the door), but occasionally, I do extract from them painful recompense—I force them to listen to excerpts from my books-in-process, and sometimes organize a class series around my current project. In preparing for this book, the dear souls endured four consecutive classes on oracles.

The classes pretty much followed the format of this book. The first dealt with my field theory of what oracles are and why they work. While preparing for the second class, I started thinking about the line, "Oracles work because they are perfect." (Ultimately, of course, everything is perfect. But you have to be God before you can really see that.) I started by asking myself, "What is something that is so perfect that every time I come in contact with it I blurt out, 'Man, that is just perfect!'"? Immediately I answered my own question: Mark Twain.

I know it sounds silly, but to me, the works, wit, and wisdom of Mark Twain are exquisite and sublime. Every time I read one of his stories or hear somebody quote him, I say to myself, "My god, that's perfect!"

I determined then and there that I would invent a Mark Twain oracle, an oracle that would not only give answers, but would do so by actually drawing the querist into a conversation with this god of literature.

It was a beautiful day, so I snatched a copy of *Tom Sawyer*, a pad of paper, and a pen, and headed for our backyard garden. I carelessly thumbed through the text, randomly stopping at a page to see what words jumped out at me. I then wrote those words down, until I had a list of eighty snippets. Back in the house, I used a spreadsheet program on my computer to box each of the quotes and arranged them so I could print them out on card stock. Then I cut them out to yield a tiny deck of *Tom Sawyer* quotation cards. I have reproduced them below (see table 7 on page 129-30), so you can copy them and create your own deck.

My next step was to devise a method of reading these cards. They really weren't suited for reading like a tarot spread, and I wanted something more conversational, just as if I were sitting in the same room chatting with Mark Twain. I decided on a simple procedure.

The dead can speak.

To consult the oracle, all you need are two simple tools: a deck of eighty Mark Twain oracle cards and two dice of different colors (I use red and green in the example below).

1. Shuffle the cards while thinking of your question.

2. When finished, set the deck on the table before you and recite the Huckleberry Finn invocation: "Devil follow corpse, cat follow devil, warts follow cat, I'm done with ye!"

3. Cut the deck with your left hand and place the bottom half on top.

4. Carefully lay out a grid of thirty-six cards (six per row, six per column, as in table 6 on page 128).

5. Put the remaining cards in a stack facedown near the grid.

6. Keeping your mind focused on your question, throw the dice.

7. Using the numbers on the dice, locate your card and read it. The green die indicates the number of the horizontal row. The red die indicates the number of the vertical column.

8. If the response doesn't make sense or you need further clarification, put that card aside and replace it with a card from the stack of forty-four cards remaining.

9. Ask your question again, but this time, treat the oracle as if you were actually having a conversation with Mark Twain himself. Feel free to say, "What's that supposed to mean?" or "By that do you mean . . . ?"

10. Repeat this process as many times as necessary, until the answer sinks home to you.

11. Enjoy!

Wait until autumn.

TABLE 6. LOCATING AN ANSWER CARD USING TWO COLORED DICE					
Use red die to find column.					
1	2	3	4	5	6
7	8	9	10	11	12
13	14	15	16	17	18
19	20	21	22	23	24
25	26	27	28	29	30
31	32	33	34	35	36

Use green die to find row.

Oh, by the way. Do you want to know what happened the first time I consulted this oracle? It was about ten minutes before people started arriving for Monday Night Magick Class and the debut of the Mark Twain oracle. I prepared everything as outlined above and did the little invocation. My first question was this:

"Is this oracle for real?"

I threw the dice.

Answer: "Well that sounds like a good way; but that ain't the way Bob Tanner done."

On a more serious note, I was demonstrating the Mark Twain oracle before a good-sized audience at PantheaCon recently. I asked for volunteers to come forward and ask the oracle questions. Two or three people came forward and asked rather light and practical questions. The oracle engaged them in Zen-like conversations that had us all laughing like crazy until it finally gave them a satisfactory answer.

Finally, one young woman came forward and asked, "Was (man's name) death a homicide or suicide?"

As you can imagine the lighthearted atmosphere in the room collapsed coldly into silence. She rolled the dice, picked the card, and read it aloud.

"The switch hovered in the air—the peril was desperate."

Nearly everybody gasped.

The young woman placed the card back down on the table. "That tells me what I want to know."

TABLE 7. ANSWER CARDS FOR THE MARK TWAIN ORACLE

1. 'Tis well. Give the countersign.	**2.** It's ever so gay!	**3.** . . . a pirate's always respected.	**4.** Run away!
5. Listen — don't talk.	**6.** Well go 'long —who's hendering you?	**7.** The picnic's for me.	**8.** It's a good lie.
9. Well that's the foolishest thing you could do.	**10.** Now you better think 'bout this a while.	**11.** Shucks, witches ain't got no power in the daytime.	**12.** It ain't any use, Huck, we're wrong again.
13. Don't Tom! It's awful.	**14.** Now where are you going to sleep?	**15.** Huck's got money.	**16.** It's an awful snug place for orgies.

Forget about it.

17. Huck, it's in the cave.	**18.** No— never mind.	**19.** It'll be over by and by, maybe.	**20.** Don't call anybody.
21. All right —go ahead— start him up.	**22.** Devil follow corpse, cat follow devil, warts follow cat, I'm done with ye!	**23.** You mustn't forget your manners.	**24.** Have the initiation.
25. I've tried it, and it don't work.	**26.** It's awful to be so tied up.	**27.** I hate them ornery sermons.	**28.** We'll drop this thing for today, and play.
29. Child you never think. You never think of anything but your own selfishness.	**30.** But shucks! Your mother won't know, and so what's the harm?	**31.** Your saying so don't make it so.	**32.** Well you said you'd do it—why don't you do it?

33. By jingo! For two cents I will do it.	34. Forty times I've said if you didn't let that jam alone I'd skin you. Hand me that switch.	35. But old fools is the biggest fools there is.	36. Can't learn old dogs new tricks, as the saying is.
37. He's full of Old Scratch.	38. Yes, I've seen whole families in the same fix.	39. . . . and anybody that'll take a dare will suck eggs.	40. I won't
41. You're a coward and a pup.	42. Don't crowd me, now; you better look out.	43. . . . It will be wisest not to reveal any of that part of their lives at present.	44. Well that sounds like a good way; but that ain't the way Bob Tanner done.
45. Oh it ain't anything.	46. You bad thing!	47. Do you love rats?	48. I'll let you chew it awhile but you must give it back to me.

Some days, you just can't make a mistake.

49. I'm going to be a clown in a circus when I grow up.	**50.** It's p'ison. That's what it is.	**51.** No answer.	**52.** Oh, lordy, I'm thankful!
53. I reckon there ain't no mistake 'bout where I'll go to. I been so wicked.	**54.** This comes of playing hookey and doing everything a feller's told not to do.	**55.** Oh lordy, lordy, lordy, I wisht I only had half your chance.	**56.** The switch hovered in the air—the peril was desperate.
57. Yes, but she ain't dead. And what's more, she's getting better, too.	**58.** This final feather broke the camel's back.	**59.** The money's in the cave!	**60.** . . . it's the snuggest hole in this country.
61. They ain't anybody as polite as robbers— you'll see that in any book.	**62.** I've a notion to skin you alive!	**63.** Well, you've done enough.	**64.** . . . don't lie —don't do it. It only makes things a hun- dred times worse.

It ain't
necessarily so.

65. I wish, now, you'd waked up when I kissed you.	**66.** The words sounded like truth.	**67.** I had a rotten bad dream last night—dreamt about rats.	**68.** My goodness, I wish I was out of this.
69. Church ain't shucks to a circus.	**70.** There's things going on at a circus all the time.	**71.** I'll whisper it. I'll whisper it ever so easy.	**72.** No reply —but sobs.
73. Hi-yi! You're up a stump, ain't you!	**74.** Hello, old chap, you got to work, hey?	**75.** Well, maybe it is, and maybe it ain't. All I know, is, it suits Tom Sawyer.	**76.** Like it? Well, I don't see why I oughtn't to like it.
77. Does a boy get a chance to whitewash a fence every day?	**78.** I'll give you the core of my apple.	**79.** . . . in order to make a man or a boy covet a thing, it is only necessary to make the thing difficult to attain.	**80.** So endeth this chronicle.

Reach out.

You're just being
paranoid.

CHAPTER 11

ASK SHAKESPEARE

Some oracle must rectify our knowledge.

—*Prospero in William Shakespeare's* The Tempest

I suppose so, but why on earth would you want to?

W^E often hear it said that the teacher learns far more from the student than the student learns from the teacher. This is certainly true in the case of the next oracle.

One week after I unveiled the Mark Twain oracle to our students, one of them, Ms. Ann Quinn, came to class armed with an original oracle that works along similar lines, but speaks with the words of William Shakespeare's most magical play, *The Tempest*. Moreover, this student outdid us all by remembering the all-important Fourth Secret Every Fortuneteller Must Know and Understand (see chapter 2):

The oracle is a superior intelligence.

She created in Shakespeare's own words a most profound and dramatic prologue and epilogue to the consultation procedure itself. These added touches ingeniously succeeded in putting us all in the mood to receive wise and witty answers to our questions from one of the most demonstrably superior intelligences who ever put pen to paper—the immortal Bard himself.

Ms. Quinn has graciously allowed me to present her inspired oracle in this book. But make no mistake. Even though a book of Shakespeare's plays may be an ordinary item in many homes, this marvelous oracle is a most *extra-*ordinary treasure.

Shakespeare's *The Tempest* is a play about a magician, Prospero, who uses his art and wisdom to manifest a good ending for all of the characters in the play. Prospero commands spirits, invokes and banishes, and works his will through his magic. It is an ideal text to use for an oracle.

Ann chose thirty-six quotes from *The Tempest* as oracular answers. These she handwrote in silver ink on one side of thirty-six cards made of dark blue paper. On the other side of each card she wrote two striking quotations from the play: "What see'st thou else in the dark backward and abysm of time?"and *"Some oracle must rectify our knowledge."*

These words actually seem to suggest that Shakespeare intended us to come to him through his marvelous poetry, for insight, as well as for diversion.

What follows is the text of the opening to the oracle. Ann is a very talented and beautiful professional flamenco dancer, and she accompanied these words with the most graceful movements and gestures. She started by standing in the center of the room facing east (toward Stratford on Avon, of course!).

"No tongue! All eyes! Be silent!"

"All hail great master, grave sir, hail!"

Probably not.

"I come to answer thy best pleasure,

be't to fly, to swim, to dive into the fire,

to ride the curled cloud—

to tread the ooze of the salt deep,

to ride on the sharp wind of the north,

to do me business in the veins of the earth . . ."

"Come forth, I say, come!"

"What see'st thou else in the dark backward and abysm of time?"

"Some oracle must rectify our knowledge."

She then spread out the thirty-six oracular cards facedown in a fan on the floor. Each of the class members then came forward, selected a card at random, and read it silently.

When we all had selected our cards, Ann ended the consultation and sent Shakespeare on his way. Again, her words were accompanied by the most beautiful and dramatic gestures.

"Here cease more questions!"

"Our revels now are ended.

These our actors, as I foretold you,

Were all spirits, and are melted into air,

Into thin air . . ."

"We are such stuff as dreams are made of,

Sorry now.
Happy later.

> And our little life is rounded with a sleep."
>
> "Then to the elements, be free!"
>
> "No tongue! All eyes! Be silent!"

When she finished and took her seat we all sat absolutely silent in stunned awe. Then everyone started talking at once, sharing the answers they had received.

One class member was comforted about a concern she was not inclined to share with the class. The Bard had answered: "By this good light, this is a very shallow monster!"

Another asked whether or not they should confront an incompetent supervisor. The answer was "Use your authority. If you cannot, give thanks you have lived so long."

As often happens with any oracle, not everyone received an answer that was understandable at the time. (The poor soul who got ". . .bite him to death, I prithee . . ." asked to draw another card.)

My question, of course, was rude and sophomoric. I asked, "Who really wrote the Shakespeare plays . . . William Shakespeare or Sir Francis Bacon?"

My answer put me soundly in my place: "I do smell all horse-piss, at which my nose is in great indignation."

I impudently selected another card that read: "At this time I will tell no tales."

Here are the thirty-six possible answers which, if you wish to use this oracle, you will want to transfer to cards as Ann did.

It's really none of your business.

1. "Keep to your cabins: you do assist the storm."

2. "Use your authority. If you cannot, give thanks you have lived so long."

3. "Be collected. No more amazement. Tell your piteous heart there's no harm done."

4. "Be of comfort."

5. "Thou shalt be as free as mountain winds."

6. "Be merry. You have cause for joy; for our escape is much beyond our loss."

7. "You rub the sore when you should bring the plaster."

8. "Go to! Away!"

9. "Hence, and bestow your luggage where you found it."

10. "My strong imagination sees a crown dropping upon your head."

11. "Thou let'st thy fortune sleep."

12. "O, out of that no hope what great hope have you."

13. "O, that you bore in mind that I do! What a sleep were this for your advancement."

14. "While you here do snoring lie, open eyed conspiracy his time doth take."

15. "Misery acquaints a man with strange bedfellows."

16. "This is a very scurvy tune."

17. "This will shake your shaking."

18. "You cannot tell who's your friend."

It's a tempest in a teapot.

19. "By this good light, this is a very shallow monster!"

20. "Some kinds of baseness are nobly undergone, and most poor matters point to rich ends"

21. "All the more it seeks to hide itself, the bigger bulk it shows."

22. "... but you'll lie like dogs, and yet say nothing neither."

23. "... bite him to death, I prithee ..."

24. "lThou shalt be lord of it."

25. "Be not afeared."

26. "Here's a maze trod indeed through forthrights and meanders."

27. "All thy vexations were but trials of thy love, and thou hast strangely stood the test."

28. "Thou liest."

29. "Well done! Avoid! No more!"

30. "I do smell all horse-piss, at which my nose is in great indignation."

31. "Let them be hunted soundly."

32. "At this time I will tell no tales."

33. "I prophesied, if a gallows were on land, this fellow could not drown."

34. "I'll deliver all, and promise you calm seas, auspicious gales, and sail so expeditious ..."

35. "My master, through his art, foresees the danger thou art in."

36. "... work not so hard ..."

CHAPTER 12

THE PENDULUM

In the hand of a trained operator, the pendulum reads exact energy patterns, which in the final analysis, is the only truth we know.

—Greg Nielsen and Joseph Polansky[1]

THE pendulum is perhaps the most powerful and mysterious divinatory tool in the fortuneteller's arsenal. It is simple to use and can perform in almost infinite ways. It is different than other oracles because it makes you, your body, and your electrical and psychic energy fields the vehicles for the oracular intelligence. It is an aspect of the art and science of radiesthesia and based upon the same principles as dowsing. By using a pendulum regularly, you become increasingly attuned to the subtle forces and more sensitive to the curious ways oracular intelligences communicate.

You don't have a pendulum?

Well, you can make one in about two minutes using stuff you have around the house. Most anything will do. A pendulum is just a weight at the end of a string. Tie a ring or earring to a thread or thin chain about eight inches long. You'll find something. If you discover you have a knack for pendulum work, you will have no difficulty finding a wide assortment of professional-quality pendulums for sale at New Age book and gift shops. I've even seen them for sale at health-food stores.

You need only spend a few moments with your pendulum to get a feel for it. Start by draping the end of the string over your index finger (pinching the end of the string down with your thumb) and letting the weight swing naturally. Then "will" it to swing in a clockwise circle. When it does, mentally inform it (or the intelligence behind it) that a clockwise swing means "yes." Repeat this little exercise a few times so that the concept of the word "yes" is connected with seeing the pendulum swing in a clockwise direction. Then do the same thing with the word "no," but linking it in your mind with a counterclockwise movement. No kidding, that's all you have to do to get started using a pendulum.

Once you're attuned to your pendulum, the things it can do for you are mind-boggling. The pendulum's potential as an oracular device is limited only by your imagination. You can even use it in combination with other oracles—selecting tarot cards or numbers to create I Ching hexagrams, etc. Use it over maps, or books, or newspapers, or (as I do in the example below) Scrabble tiles.

While preparing material for this chapter, I thought it would be nice to chronicle the events of a brief pendulum operation, so I got out my pendulum (a nice brass miniature surveyor's plumb), settled into my comfy chair, and quietly chanted the name of Ganesha 108 times to the tune of *Pop Goes the Weasel*. The chanting seemed to put me in a creative state of mind, because I suddenly got an exciting idea.

It occurred to me that the power of the pendulum could be amplified if I

Ask two more times and pick the answer you like best.

tied its string to the end of my magick wand (an especially consecrated length of almond wood that I fashioned thirty years ago for use in my magical operations). I thought it could prove very handy to be able to point the wand (with the pendulum dangling from the tip) in certain directions and ask things like, "Did I leave my car keys in this direction?". So I asked: "Will tying the pendulum to the end of my magick wand make communication with you easier and stronger?" The pendulum swung in a clockwise motion, indicating "yes."

I got up and fetched my wand and removed it from its red satin bag. I tied the pendulum string to one end of my wand, which I had carved to represent its female, or negatively charged, end. "Is this the end I should tie it to?" The pendulum was motionless, a rare event.

I then tied the string to the male, or positively charged, end. "Is this the end I should tie it to?" The pendulum swung strongly in a clockwise direction— "yes."

Okay, we're ready to start. But I still hadn't thought of a question to ask.

Then the thought occurred to me that, in all the years I had used the pendulum, I had never asked the spiritual intelligence working through the pendulum its name. So I asked the following questions:

"Are you the intelligence I communicate with when I use the pendulum?" The pendulum immediately swung strongly clockwise—"yes."

"Do you have a name?" Clockwise again—"yes."

"Will you tell me your name?" Again, clockwise—"yes."

"Is your name written in a book in this house?" Again, clockwise—"yes."

This was great news because, as I mentioned in chapter 4, an answer from

A message
is coming.

a book is the most effective way an oracle can give a clear response. But to make sure there wasn't some kind of loophole to this answer, I continued cautiously:

"Would I be able to find your name in a book in this house?"
   Clockwise—"yes"

"Is it in a book downstairs?" Counterclockwise—"no." Oops!

"Is it in a book upstairs in the loft?" "Yes." That's better.

"If I go upstairs with the wand and pendulum will you point out the book? "No." Ouch! Now I was stuck.

I thought for a moment then asked, "Will you spell your name for me?"
   "Yes." Now we're getting somewhere.

I got up to get paper and pencil to make an alphabet chart, but then it occurred to me that, out in the garage, was a game of Scrabble containing a whole bag of alphabet tiles. I went out to the garage, got the bag of tiles, and returned to my comfy chair. I picked out twenty-six tiles representing the entire alphabet. (I didn't stop to consider that the name could contain more than one of the same letter.) I laid the tiles face down on a little footstool Constance had made with her talented little hands, and swirled them around. Then I held it over each tile and asked, "Is this a letter in your name?" I must have been quite a sight—a big gray-haired man holding what looked like a tiny fishing pole over a bunch of Scrabble tiles.

It took longer than I expected, but I finally wound up with five tiles that evoked enthusiastic "yes" responses. I turned them over in the order they were chosen.

PHOCU

I sounded the letters out and was not happy with the message. I lifted my oracular fishing pole.

"Are you saying to me 'F*** you!?'" "Yes." "Is 'F*** you' your name?" "No."

I knew then that I was dealing with an intelligence with a impish sense of humor. Just to make sure I asked, "Are you sure these letters spell your name?" The pendulum confirmed it.

I turned the five tiles face down and swirled them around to shuffle them. Then, one by one, I held the pendulum over them and systematically asked, "Is this the first letter of your name?" "Is this the second letter of your name?" for all five tiles. Before I turned them over, I asked one more time, "Is this your name?" to which the pendulum replied "yes."

POCUH

I was pleased that the consonants didn't bunch up, but it sure was a strange-looking word. I held the pendulum over the tiles while I sounded out different pronunciations.

"Pock oo?""No."

"Poke ah?" Again, "no."

"Pooc uh?" "Yes." Finally!

"Really? Pronounced Pooka, like Harvey, the invisible six-foot-tall rabbit
  in the movie?" "Yes."

So there it was. The name of my oracular pendulum friend is spelled Pocuh and pronounced "Pooka." But why did it choose those particular letters? I had to ask.

"Is your name more correctly spelled Pooka?" Clockwise—"yes."

"If there had been another "O" tile to choose from, would you have

Is this trip necessary?

selected it also?" "No." So much for that theory!

"Is that because you wanted to first say to me, 'F*** you'"? "Yes." Bingo!

I thanked my Puckish[2] friend and put the pendulum and my wand away for the day.

This better not be an important question.

CHAPTER 13

THE I CHING

Nothing endures but change.

—*Heraclitus*

AND so we come to the final chapter of *The Book of Ordinary Oracles*. I hope you've enjoyed yourself and want to investigate this fascinating subject further. I confess that the final oracle we'll discuss is hardly "ordinary." As a matter of fact, even though the I Ching could be considered an industrial strength, super-sized deluxe version of Ko-Ween, it is one of the most extraordinary oracles in the world. True to the theme of this book, however, I'll show you how to consult this oracle using some very ordinary things you probably have around the house.

The first time I consulted the I Ching, I followed the complex directions of the traditional Chinese yarrow-stalk method (clumsily manipulating forty-nine lengths of tiny wooden doweling instead of the traditional yarrow stalks). My first question was, "I Ching, what are you to me?" After the brief traditional ceremony and about a half hour of fumbling with the sticks, I

This is something only you can accomplish.

received my answer. I looked it up in my John Blofeld edition.[1]

Question: "I Ching, what are you to me?"

Answer: Hexagram #14 Great Possessions

            He who possesses much—supreme success!

Time seemed to stop when I read those words. I no longer felt alone in the room. The atmosphere around me was warm and serene, and I felt that I was in the loving presence of the Supreme Intelligence of the universe in the form of a Chinese sage. I knew without a shadow of a doubt that, from that moment forward, the I Ching would indeed be one of the great possessions of my life.

The I Ching is without a doubt the oldest and most venerable oracle in the world. How old is it? Would you believe 6,000 years old? At least its roots can be traced back that far—back to China's legendary first emperor, Fu Hsi (4000 B.C.).

Fu Hsi was quite a character. After a busy morning of breaking his unwashed prehistoric hunting-gathering neighbors of their nasty habit of eating each other, this guy turned around and taught them how to plant crops, net fish, domesticate animals, grow silkworms, speak in complete sentences, and compute the proper amount to tip the waitress.

After all that, he still had time to create the Tai Chi philosophy, which, after 6,000 years, is still the foundation of Eastern thought—from Tai-Chi to the martial arts, from Zen to Feng Shui (not to mention the unified field and superstring theories of modern physics).

Fu Hsi's greatest invention, however, was the concept of Ko-Ween. Okay— that's not exactly true. He didn't call it Ko-Ween; he called it "yin and yang."

Yes (and I hope you're ready for it).

Like the Oracle of Ko-Ween, the concept of yin and yang easily accommodates the notion of heads and tails. Potentially, however, it is infinitely more meaningful, encompassing the cosmic duality of all nature, existence, and consciousness. Actually nature, existence, and consciousness are the same thing, but you only realize that when you see beyond duality! Until then, you are faced with two very fundamental concepts that seem to be the key to everything: negative (yin) and positive (yang).

Fu Hsi symbolized yin as a broken line (━ ━) and yang as an unbroken line (━━━). Thus yin-yang is exactly the same as Ko-Ween's heads and tails. In fact, it may be that, at the very beginning, that's just how it was treated— as a simple means for answering yes-no questions.

I can imagine the early experiments. (Cue the Gu Zheng music.) Ancient Chinese villagers huddle around a communal fire to consult the oracle. They ask the question: "Will there be victory if we attack the neighboring village tomorrow?" With great solemnity, they throw an empty tortoise shell in the fire and wait for it to crack. (That's probably what they really did at first.). As they wait, they silently concentrate on their question, hoping the gods will hear their thoughts and affect the cracking of the shell. Finally, the shell cracks and they pull it out of the fire to examine it. It is cracked in such a way that they conclude the answer is: "━━━"—yang.

The villagers take this as a "yes," because yang is unbroken, strong, and aggressive. The next day, they gird their loins and confidently attack the neighboring village. Unfortunately, they get their butts trounced and have to retreat. After nursing their wounds, the survivors come together again. They figure that the oracle answered correctly, but they just interpreted it incorrectly. The strong unbroken line of the oracle was trying to tell them their enemy would be too strong to overcome.

They agree they should be more careful with the wording of their questions, and that they are likely to get more accurate answers if they use two tortoise shells. This time, they word their question more carefully: two yangs will encourage them to attack; two yins will discourage them from attacking. If the first one is yang and the second yin, that will mean, "probably yes." But if the first one is yin and the second yang, that will mean, "probably no."

TABLE 8. DISTRIBUTION OF YES/NO ANSWERS

Yes	Probably Yes	Probably No	No
▬▬▬	▬ ▬	▬ ▬	▬ ▬
▬▬▬	▬▬▬	▬ ▬	▬ ▬

(Note: Columns are read from the bottom up.)

Understandably, it was the "probablys" everyone had a problem with, and, after a couple of more defeats at the hands of the warriors of the neighboring village, the survivors limped once more into oracle circle. For the first time in human history, one of them spoke the historic words that would be uttered by every kid in the future who ever lost a sandlot coin toss . . . "Best two out of three?"

At that moment the I Ching was born.

THE EIGHT TRIGRAMS AND THE SIXTY-FOUR HEXAGRAMS

Tossing three tortoise shells in the fire might have been more expensive, but it added a sublime dimension to the oracular process. First of all, it allowed for eight possible fundamental answers. Each answer—composed of the results from the three turtle-shell tosses—is called a trigram.

TABLE 9. THE EIGHT TRIGRAMS

Obviously this created more shades of "probably" to contemplate, but contemplation is a good thing where oracles are concerned. Besides, as time passed, the trigrams took on special meanings of their own—meanings relating to life, nature, and spiritual matters.

Later, commentator King Wen tinkered a bit with Fu Hsi's original arrangement of the trigrams and gave us the names and general meanings we have today. The shapes of the individual trigrams are also suggestive of images, which adds yet another dimension to the process that is completely absent in simple coin flipping. In English, the eight trigrams translate roughly as follows:

TABLE 10. ENGLISH TRANSLATIONS OF THE EIGHT TRIGRAMS

Heaven	Thunder	Water	Mountain	Earth	Wind	Fire	Lake

I don't know. Read your cards.

As the years passed, sages (with obviously far too much time on their hands) decided to double the trigrams by stacking one on top of another, giving us sixty-four hexagrams—each hexagram made up of the results from three turtle shells being tossed six times—with more complex meanings and images: heaven over water, lake over fire, mountain over thunder, etc. Even Confucius got in on the act and wrote extensive commentaries on the hexagrams and individual lines. When he was ninety years old (so the story goes), he told his friends that, if he had another ninety years to live, he would spend it all studying the I Ching.

Today, there are many translations of the I Ching and many commentaries available. Some are easier to understand than others, but all are based ultimately on the disarmingly simple meanings of six lines (either broken or unbroken), how they are arranged, and how they change. What do I mean by *change*?

THE BOOK OF CHANGES

As we learned in chapter 2, the fortuneteller's third secret is that there is no future to look into. There is only the Great Now. To this, the divinatory gods of the I Ching would add: ". . . and the Great Now is in an eternal state of change."

The idea that life is in a state of constant change literally brought life to the I Ching oracle and eventually gave it its name, *The Book of Changes*. In the I Ching, "being" is a continual process of "becoming." If we must speak in terms of past-present-future, then we have to say that everything is different from what it was a moment ago, and will be different again a moment from now. How, then, can we hope to determine future events or conditions if all we have to work with is a now that is continually passing away?

Before the days of computer-generated animation, professional cartoonists first drew sketches of action sequences on a large pad of paper. They began from the back of the pad and worked forward so that, as they flipped the pages from back to front, they could see (in a very primitive way) the movement of the figures. Let's say the first drawing shows two men facing each other; the second drawing shows both of the men closer to each other with their right arms raised; the third shows the two men shaking hands. Each drawing is a snapshot of the Great Now. The first drawing gives us some information—two men facing each other. We don't know if they are friendly, if they are approaching each other or taking their leave.

The next snapshot shows change. The men are close to each other and have raised their arms. By analyzing the change, we learn much more about the situation. We know what direction they are moving; we know that they each are likely to take some action with or against each other. They could be getting ready to hug or hit each other.

But the changes shown in the third snapshot give us complex and tangible information that is easy to interpret. That's how the I Ching answers our questions—by giving us snapshots of the Great Now that reveal, by their movement, the direction in which the situation is changing. This allows us to intuit what will come next.

When we consult the I Ching, we usually receive an answer in three parts:

1. The initial hexagram that usually indicates the general conditions.
2. The line or lines within the initial hexagram that is (are) in the process of moving into its (their) opposite(s). In other words, one or more of the lines have gotten so old ("old yin" or "old yang") that they are about to change—a yin into a yang, or a yang into a yin.

These are called "moving lines," and they each have a meaning and commentary. (It is possible to get a hexagram with no moving lines, or one, two, three, four, five, or six moving lines. We'll see in a moment how that can be.)

3. Finally, once the moving lines have changed, a new hexagram is formed, creating the third snapshot.

Here's an example. I asked a question: "What must I do to advance my life's work?" Then I tossed three coins (a more sophisticated version of turtle shells) six times and used the chart at the end of this chapter to determine the hexagram that was my answer (see the Three-Coin Method on page 161 for more explanation). The coin toss resulted in an initial hexagram (#17, which is called "Following") and four moving lines (counting from the bottom, 1, 2, 4, and 5). Then I transformed the moving lines into their opposites and got the final hexagram (#7, which is called "The Army").

TABLE 11. INITIAL HEXAGRAM, MOVING LINES, AND RESULTING HEXAGRAM

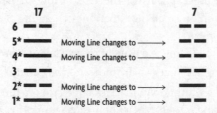

Now it's time to consult the text to get my answer. The text you see here is taken from my own paraphrased interpretation of the sixty-four hexagrams and all 384 moving lines, which I've narcissistically titled the "I Ching of Mi-Lo." It's obviously not a bona fide translation, but it is a rephrasing of the text based on my thirty-five years of personal observations and experiences with the I Ching. I've included the entire text of the I Ching of Mi-Lo for your amusement at the end of this book. If you really want to learn more about the I Ching, I strongly advise you to become acquainted with a good scholarly translation, such as the one by Richard Wilhelm and rendered into English by Cary F. Baynes. It has a wonderful foreword by Carl Jung and is a real treasure for lovers of the I Ching.[2]

First, I read the general meaning of Hexagram #17, "Following":

> "To prepare to rule, first learn to serve. If you're a true ruler
>   it will seem like a rest."

Not bad—good advice, but kind of fortune-cookie-ish. But I really get down to specific advice when I read the text for each of the four moving lines. Listen to this:

- Moving line in the first position (bottom) reads "You'll never learn anything hanging around your yes-men and groupies. Get out and mingle."

- Moving line in the second position reads: "Good-for-nothing old chums chase away cool new people."

- Moving line in the fourth position reads: "Don't get hooked on your fawning groupies."

- Moving line in the fifth position reads: "Pursue excellence. Make it your magnetic north."

Sit back, relax, and enjoy your flight.

Now that's specific in-my-face advice! I'm almost sorry I asked. Now, the only thing that remains is to create the final hexagram by changing those four moving lines into their opposites. The final hexagram should indicate the direction all this is heading. The final hexagram, # 7—"The Army"—reads:

> "Wisdom, guts and tenacity. Do you have what it takes to be
> a good general?"

> As you can see, the I Ching doesn't pull its punches.

CONSULTING THE I CHING

Now it's time to learn how to consult the I Ching. I'm going to outline four very quick and easy procedures that use things you have around the house. I don't want to discourage you, however, from learning and mastering the traditional Chinese method. It is pretty involved and requires the use of fifty yarrow stalks, which I'm sure many of you don't have around the house. The procedure takes about fifteen minutes to perform, during which time you're expected to keep your mind concentrated on the question. I use this method when reading for myself, and I encourage anyone who feels spiritually drawn to the I Ching to obtain John Blofeld's *I Ching (The Book of Changes): A New Translation of the Ancient Chinese Text with Detailed Instructions for Its Practical Use in Divination*[3] or one of several excellent scholarly texts available that can help you research and master the ceremony in its entirety.

The Popsicle-stick Method

This method is by far the fastest and easiest method of consulting the I Ching. If you are a beginner, I recommend that you use this method while getting acquainted with the oracle and how it answers questions. Its singular advan-

The seat belt signs are lit.

tage (and drawback), as you will soon see, is that each throw always produces a hexagram with one (and only one) moving line. This method does not approximate the odds for the traditional yarrow stalk or coin method, but it always assures a classic three-part answer and simplifies the interpretation process immensely.

Take six Popsicle sticks, tongue depressors, or any other identical flat sticks of equal length. Paint, stain, or otherwise make one stick a different color or shade. This unique stick will represent the moving line.

Draw or paint a vertical stripe down the center of one side of each of the six sticks. The side of the stick without the stripe represents a yang, or unbroken, line; the side with the stripe represents a yin, or broken, line.

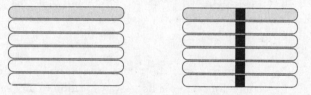

Front side of the stick (left); back side of the stick (right).

After composing your question and invoking the deity or Superior Intelligence of your choice, close your eyes and "shuffle" the sticks. When the spirit moves you, gently toss the sticks on the table or floor before you. Open you eyes and create the hexagram by placing the stick that falls nearest you on the bottom and building your way up.

Please return to your seat.

Use table 4 on page 200 to locate your hexagram. (The top trigram is found on the top row of the chart; the bottom trigram on the left hand column.) Turn to the corresponding text in the I Ching of Mi-Lo (see page 167) and read the comments for the hexagram.

Next, read the comments for the one moving line, ignoring the comments for the other lines. Finally, flip over the moving-line stick to create the second hexagram of your answer. Again, locate your new hexagram in table 12 on page 00 and read the text in the I Ching of Mi-Lo. (Don't read any of the moving lines for this second hexagram.)

Chopped-Up Chopstick Method

This method is just as easy to use as the method that uses popsicle sticks and more closely approximates the odds of the traditional methods. It provides the possibility of receiving no moving lines, or as many as six. It takes a little more time to prepare the sticks, but I think you'll be very pleased with the results.

Take six bamboo Chinese-style chopsticks. If you don't have these around the house, they can be found in the housewares section of any supermarket. They are very inexpensive. Approximately one half of each chopstick (the end you use to pick up food) is rounded. The other half, however, is squared. Use the square section to create your I Ching sticks.

Cut each of the six chopsticks in two at a point just before the rounded sections starts and discard the rounded pieces. You are left with six elongated bamboo "dice," each of which you will customize in the same way.

1. Lay the blank die horizontally in front of you and draw, paint, or carve a vertical line down the center. This represents the yin side of the die (see figure below).

The yin side.

2. Gently roll the die one-quarter rotation toward you and draw, paint, or carve two vertical lines that straddle your original mark (see figure below). This represents the old yin side of the die (a moving yin that will change into a yang).

Old yin side.

3. Gently roll the die another quarter rotation toward you. Leave this side blank (see figure below). It represents the yang side of the die (the opposite of the yin side).

The yang side.

4. Roll the die a quarter turn toward you one more time. Draw, paint, or carve two vertical lines toward the ends of the stick (see figure below). This represents the old yang side of the die (a moving yang that will change into a yin). It should be on the opposite side of the die from the old yin.

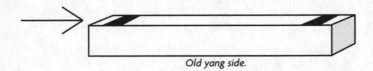

Old yang side.

When you are finished, the stick should have a yin on one side and a yang on the opposite side, and an old yin on one side and an old yang on the other.

Do this to all six sticks and you'll be rewarded with a beautiful set of I Ching sticks capable of generating highly detailed answers. Compose your question, toss your chopped-up chopsticks, use Table 4 on page 200 to determine your hexagram, and consult the I Ching of Mi-Lo exactly as you did in the popsicle-stick method (see page 156).

Three-Coin Method

This method is perhaps the most popular of all. It is very easy to use and most nearly approximates the odds of the traditional yarrow stalk ceremony.

Take three coins of any denomination or style (so long as they each have an obvious "heads" and an obvious "tails." Shake them in your hands, or use a small jar or cup. Throw them before you on the floor or a table. It doesn't matter where they land in proximity to you. All that matters is how many land as heads and how many land as tails. Use table 12 (see page 162) to determine if your throw was a yang or a yin, or an old yang or an old yin. This is how you determine the first (bottom) line of your hexagram. Write down the result of this throw. Throw the coins five more times to build up your hexagram from the bottom to the top.

Use table 4 on page 200 to determine the number of the initial hexagram, then read its overall meaning, the meaning of its moving lines, and the text meaning only of the resulting second hexagram in the I Ching of Mi-Lo (see page 167). It's as simple as that!

Silence is golden . . . and your best bet.

TABLE 12. THROW OF THREE COINS				
○○●	Yang	——		
●●○	Yin	— —		
●●●	Old Yang	——	Changing to	— —
○○○	Old Yin	— —	Changing to	——

Dice Method

By using a single die, or two, three, or six dice, you can easily and quickly create a hexagram with no moving lines, or as many as six. Table 3 gives you the values (see below).

Compose your question as usual. Then roll one die six times, or two dice three times, or six dice once to create the hexagram. Use table 4 to determine your hexagram and consult the I Ching of Mi-Lo exactly as in the other methods.

TABLE 13. THROW OF A SINGLE DIE				
1	Old Yang	——	Changing to	— —
2	Yin	— —		
3	Yang	——		
4	Yin	— —		
5	Yang	——		
6	Old Yin	— —	Changing to	——

No matter which technique I use to generate my hexagram and moving lines, I find that the I Ching gives me the clearest, wisest, most easy-to-understand answers to my sincere questions. Have a question right now? Give it a try.

Revenge is a dish best served cold.

SO MANY ORACLES, SO LITTLE TIME

News comes on flying wings.

WELL, we've come to the end of the space allowed us for this little book. I hope you've enjoyed your read and have come away with a deeper appreciation of your own oracular abilities. There are so many more ordinary oracles I wanted to talk about: the Marble Oracle, which requires a bit of knowledge of astrology; the First Person through the Door Oracle, where the first words spoken by the next person to enter the room carry the answer; and the Family Photo Oracle, where you address your question to a family member who isn't present (or even alive for that matter) and then comb through old photo albums until you find their picture and discover your answer in elements of the photograph.

But we have to stop somewhere, so just let me say that I hope you get the picture, too. Everything we observe, whether it's an objective phenomenon outside ourselves or a subjective thought or impression inside ourselves, is a direct communication from the Superior Intelligence to our souls. That's pretty heavy when you think about it, and I'll be the first one to confess that I'm not as yet ready to listen to that voice twenty-four hours a day. It takes the inhibitions of an insane person or the spiritual integrity of a saint to do that.

But as long as we keep ourselves away from the mental institution or the martyr's stake I think most of us would agree that we'd all be wiser, healthier, and happier if we listened to that voice a little more often. After all, it's the voice of the most extraordinary oracle in the universe—you.

The end of the world isn't always the end of the world.

THE I CHING OF MI-LO

A Highly Personal, Mildly Vulgar, and Not-at-All Scholarly Rendering of the Classic Text

by Lon Mi-Lo DuQuette

1.
THE CREATIVE

Creative effort brings success.
Build your strength and stamina.

━━━ They'll be sorry they messed with you!
━━━ The problem is obvious to everyone. Seek expert advice.
━━━ You'll make it. But whatever you do . . . don't look down!
━━━ Create all day. Worry all night. Things will eventually work out.
━━━ The problem's right under your nose. Seek expert advice.
━━━ There's a hidden problem. Don't act.

2.
THE RECEPTIVE

Don't lead. Follow.
Quietly!

━ ━ A nasty fight. Both get hurt.
━ ━ A true leader doesn't need to overdress.
━ ━ At the moment, maintaining a low profile is not good enough. Become invisible!
━ ━ Continue to glow brightly, but for now . . . hide your light.
━ ━ Develop like natural things, without worry or lust of result.
━ ━ The first signs of decay are showing.

You're going to
need a lot of help.

3.
DIFFICULTY AT THE BEGINNING

Birth pains; growing pains.
Hang in there and round up some helpers.

━━ ━━ Ouch! This mess is too much for most folks to handle—you too, probably.

━━━━ Others can't understand your big dream. Let them help with the small ones that lead there.

━━ ━━ Act now—even if you have to swallow a little pride.

━━ ━━ It's better to throw in the towel than to go off half-cocked.

━━ ━━ Unexpected help flops! Sorry! This is going to take longer than you think.

━━━━ Stay focused, but it's still too early to force things. Friends help.

4.
YOUTHFUL FOLLY

It's OK to act like a jerk when you're a kid.
Don't press your luck, and don't ask the oracle this stupid question again.

━━━━ You idiot! You won't get away unpunished.

━━ ━━ Your childlike ignorance attracts wise instruction.

━━ ━━ It's a really dumb idea. Give it up!

━━ ━━ Nobody respects a kiss-up.

━━━━ Tolerate fools just enough to take control of them . . . and then the ship.

━━ ━━ Take control of yourself, but still have fun.

Try again in
two hours.

5.
WAITING

Be calm.
Have patience, even if things are getting hairy.

— — All looks lost. But wait . . . a miracle!

——— Eat. Drink. Enjoy this short break from your struggles.

— — Extreme danger. Sorry. Anything you try to do will just make things worse.

——— Attacking prematurely will alert the enemy.

——— There is gossip. Challenging it will only create more. Seal thy lips.

——— Save your energy. Danger's not on your doorstep yet. Go about your business until it arrives.

6.
CONFLICT

Civil lawsuit. Even if you're absolutely correct, meet your enemy halfway.
If the hassle hasn't really started, there may still be a way around it.

——— You win the prize! But wait . . . someone just stole your trophy and is now hitting you with it.

——— Be happy to submit to arbitration.

——— You're on the wrong side and you know it. Do the right thing.

— — Do the job well and let others take the glory.

——— Now maybe is a good time to turn tail and go home.

— — Let the matter drop (especially if he's bigger than you).

Now you're
getting greedy.

7.
THE ARMY

Wisdom, guts, and tenacity.
Do you have what it takes to be a good general?

▬ ▬ Victory! Reward the troops (but not with government jobs). Then send 'em home.

▬ ▬ You've been invaded. Now's the time to hatch a smart plan and really kick some butt!

▬ ▬ Retreat. The opposition is too strong. Save your troops so you can fight another day.

▬ ▬ If your troops (instead of you) are calling the shots, all is lost.

▬▬▬ Jump in the trenches and fight shoulder-to-shoulder with your troops. Your superiors will notice.

▬ ▬ Is this cause really just? Is everyone really on board? If not, you're going to get burned—badly.

8.
HOLDING TOGETHER

A new organization can accomplish great things.
Go ahead. Ask the oracle once again if you have what it takes to lead it.

▬ ▬ Too late. You've missed your chance to pull this thing together.

▬▬▬ No need to brownnose or bully anyone. Your best helpers will show up voluntarily.

▬ ▬ Proudly show your support of this guy. (But keep an eye on him just the same.)

▬ ▬ Some very wrong people are in the organization. It's disaster if you don't dump them now.

▬ ▬ Don't come off as if you're running for public office. It's so obvious to your coworkers.

▬ ▬ Stay sincere and all will be cool.

It will feel so good when it stops.

9.
THE TAMING POWER OF THE SMALL

Things are way too hairy for drastic action.
Little things can be done, and a light touch will be required.

You've been successful so far. Now don't push your luck any further.
You are and have a good friend. That makes both of you rich.
You're in a truly dangerous spot, but if you stay cool, you won't get hurt.
Bad move! You've pushed too hard too early!
Others can see the handwriting on the wall. They're backing off. Better join them.
Lighten up and back off. Don't try to take things by force.

10.
TREADING

You're riding a tiger.
Enjoy the ride, but for heaven's sake, be polite.

Success! But only time will tell if it was the right thing to do.
You'll make it if you don't lose sight of the danger.
I know it's scary, but keep moving.
Ouch! Sorry. You're in way over your head.
Don't get caught up in things. Pretend you're a hermit. Enjoy the simple way.
Keep it (and yourself) very *very* simple.

Has your luggage been in your control the whole time?

II.
PEACE

Peace. Prosperity. All's in proper relation.
Good stuff coming. Bad stuff going. Is everybody happy? Yes!

▬▬ Your world is falling apart. If you try to resist, things will just get worse.
▬▬ Modest princess marries modest commoner—make each other happy.
▬▬ Don't flaunt your wealth or good fortune.
▬▬ Decline is inevitable. It's the law. Resist if you want to. It won't change the law.
▬▬ Good fellowship? Yes! Cliques and factions? No!
▬▬ The time is ripe. Get out there right now. It's possible to do great things.

12.
STANDSTILL

Disorder. Stagnation. Nothing's in proper relation.
Bad stuff coming. Good stuff going. Is anybody happy? Yes, lazy jerks!

▬▬ The standstill has come to an end—thanks to your fine efforts.
▬▬ A savior arrives! But don't get so excited that you forget the mess you've come out of.
▬▬ This mess is about to improve. Do you feel called to help make it happen?
▬▬ The guy at the top is an unworthy idiot. He's starting to realize that. That's good.
▬▬ Flatterers are everywhere and getting their way. Don't hang out with them.
▬▬ It's time to hang it up and salvage whatever scraps of dignity you have left.

No, but not the way you expect.

13.
FELLOWSHIP WITH MEN

A convention. A conference. A movement.
Orderliness within diversity.

—— Pragmatic fellowship. Not warm and fuzzy. Not everyone included.
—— Old adversaries are true friends at heart.
—— The quarrel may be coming to an end. At least the attacks have stopped.
—— Mistrust and paranoia. The longer this lasts, the worse it's going to get.
— — Egos breed splinter groups. Eventual embarrassment.
—— Be of one accord and don't make any secret deals.

14.
POSSESSION IN GREAT MEASURE

This is a golden moment. How lucky can you get?
You hold a treasure in your hands.

—— You're really blessed. Be cool and continue to deserve it.
— — People like you because you're truly sincere. Now don't be rude and ruin everything.
—— So what if the grass is greener next door?
—— Show some class. Be generous and philanthropic. You can't take it with you.
—— Good friends help you spread the wealth.
—— You haven't yet had a chance to make mistakes. Don't get complacent.

Has a stranger given you anything to carry on board?

15.
MODESTY

Reduce what you have too much of.
Add to what you have too little of.

— — First pull yourself together. Then pull your supporters together. Then act!

— — You can still remain modest while thoroughly kicking somebody's butt.

— — Be so modest you don't even look modest.

—— Be a star; don't just act like one. Folks like to throw stuff at pretentious jerks.

— — When you become so modest it actually shows in your behavior; nothing can stop you.

— — Don't get big-headed, even when you're really important and have really important stuff to do.

16.
ENTHUSIASM

Ah! The tension is eased.
Cheerful helpers fall in on cue, like the chorus line in an old MGM musical.

— — The party's over. You're sick, sad, and perhaps a little wiser?

— — Feel as if you're suffocating? Who knows—that condition may be the only thing keeping you alive.

—— You're the *man! (woman!)* You love your buds, and your buds love you.

— — The party stopped being fun a long time ago—and still you don't go home.

— — Be firm. Be the guy who knows exactly the right moment to leave the party.

— — A name-dropping snob spoils it for everyone.

Get it in writing.

17.
FOLLOWING

To prepare to rule, first learn to serve.
If you're a true ruler, it will seem like a rest.
— — Headline: "Retired Guru Returns to Teach Persistent and Promising Student."
——— Pursue excellence. Make it your magnetic north.
——— Don't get hooked on your fawning groupies.
— — Cool new friends chase away good-for-nothing old chums. Good riddance!
— — Good-for-nothing old chums chase away cool new people.
——— You'll never learn anything hanging around your yes-men and groupies.
Get out and mingle.

18.
WORK ON WHAT HAS BEEN SPOILED (DECAY)

What somebody ruined, somebody can fix.
Study the cause. Fix it. Then watch it for a while to make sure it works.
——— Spiritual enlightenment and withdrawal from the mundane world is indicated.
— — The source of the decay is far in the past. You and your friends can still do damage control.
— — The source of the decay is far in the past. Stop it now or somebody's really going to be embarrassed.
——— Perhaps a little too much revolution—a few ruffled feathers. Don't worry. They'll get over it.
——— There's decay because someone was too weak to stop it. Try to fix it without humiliating them.
— — Old-fashioned ways are starting to stink. A cautious revolution is called for.

Wait until summer.

19.
APPROACH

Success is a certainty.
Make hay while the Sun shines. It won't last forever.

▬ ▬ Headline: "Retired Saint Still Enjoys Volunteer Work."
▬ ▬ Now that you're a star, get a good manager and a good agent. Then let them do their jobs.
▬ ▬ A powerful sugardaddy takes a liking to you.
▬ ▬ Resting on your laurels causes trouble. There still may be time to snap out of it.
▬▬▬ This is your big break! Be true to yourself and enjoy the ride.
▬▬▬ You've caught the eye of the movers and shakers. Kid, this may be your big break.

20.
CONTEMPLATION (VIEW)

Think long and hard.
Regular tours of inspection are helpful.

▬▬▬ Headline: "Egoless Saint Thinks about Life. Says 'It's Great!'"
▬▬▬ Think how you're affecting the world. Is it good?
▬ ▬ This guy knows his stuff. Make him welcome and let him do his stuff.
▬ ▬ Reflective thinking reveals others to you, you to others, but most importantly, you to yourself.
▬ ▬ Narrow thinking keeps small people small.
▬ ▬ Shallow thinking won't get you beyond fads and fashion.

A tarot card will answer. Use two dice.

21.
BITING THROUGH

**Criminal lawsuit. Tattletale traitor must be busted and punished.
Throw the book at him—but nothing else.**

—— This guy's a hopeless case. He'll never reform. Life without parole—in solitary!

— — The case is complicated, but guilt is obvious.

—— Watch out. The bad guys have powerful friends. Be hard as nails and twice as sharp.

— — The wrong guy's been asked to execute punishment. This annoys everyone. So what?

— — Open-and-shut case. Guilty as charged (probably more). Lock him up and throw away the key.

—— First offence earns a slap on the wrist. Learn your lesson and change your ways.

22.
GRACE

Ah! You feel sensitive and mellow—the perfect mood to do small things that please the eye and heart. However, it's not the correct mood to be in when you need to make earthshaking decisions.

—— Ornaments and accessories are no longer necessary. Perfect form is perfectly perfect.

— — Goodbye world of shallow luxury. Fancy gifts for your new enlightened friends are unnecessary.

— — A good friend reminds you to keep it simple.

—— Life is sweet. Beautiful surroundings, good friends, good wine. Now's not the time to get sloppy.

— — A jerk in an expensive Italian suit is still a jerk.

—— The limo may be available, but at this point in your career, you really need to walk.

War is hell.

23.
SPLITTING APART

Collapse. The jerks are about to take over completely.
Don't move. Don't act. There's nothing you can do. There's nothing you should do.

—— Things are as bad as they're going to get. Evil has destroyed even itself. Jerks self-destruct.

— — Things look bad, but the cavalry comes to the rescue.

— — Ouch! You get hurt. End of story.

— — Can't beat 'em? Join 'em! (but not in your heart). It's cool to be a secret agent.

— — You're losing sleep over this one (and with good reason). Don't fight 'em head-on. Adjust.

— — Stupid enemies are coming out of the woodwork, knocking off your friends right and left.

24.
RETURN

The long night is over. Here comes the Sun! Man! That feels good!
If you handle this new feeling with care, like a sprouting seed, it will grow strong.

— — You were a stubborn idiot and didn't return in time. This will mess you up for years.

— — Hey! Apologize if you're wrong. It will make everyone feel good—especially you.

— — You find yourself on a road trip with idiots. Go home alone.

— — You're being a good boy (girl) about half of the time. That can be dangerous. Work on that.

— — You've a decision to make. Get control of yourself. How would your heroes act?

—— A little backsliding is inevitable. Catch yourself before you go too far and get back with the program.

Swallow your pride.

25.
INNOCENCE (THE UNEXPECTED)

Nature has made you good. Correct behavior is just being able to act naturally. Act unnaturally and you'll find yourself in deep doo-doo.

—— Innocence doesn't mean thoughtlessness. Don't thoughtlessly push this situation.

—— A big problem crops up. If it's not your fault, it will pass.

—— You're really cool by nature. You can't go wrong by being true to your own nature.

— — Innocence is one thing. Naiveté is another. Someone's getting ready to rip you off.

— — Keep your mind on the work. Don't count your chickens before they hatch.

—— Follow the first impulse of your heart.

26.
THE TAMING POWER OF THE GREAT

Get out of the house and conquer the world. But first broaden yourself. Read the classics. Study history—then make history.

—— The obstacles are gone. Now get out there and change the world!

— — Don't try to disarm a madman. Make him harmless by curing his madness.

— — Stay on top of things. You can head off potential problems.

—— Now's the time to *charge!* Keep one hand on the wheel, one hand on your gun.

—— Don't even think about resisting this problem. The only thing you can do is wait.

—— The obstacle in your way is too big. Don't push it. Stay calm. Wait for the right moment.

27.
THE CORNERS OF THE MOUTH (PROVIDING NOURISHMENT)

Observe what comes out of your mouth and what goes into it.
You are what you eat . . . and what you say.

—— Always remember that you nourish the world around you.

— — Your "feed-the-hungry" crusade's a flop. To know what hunger is, listen to a hungry person.

— — Like a starving tiger, hunt for people who can help you change the world.

— — Junk food. Junk thoughts. Both are addictive; both with kill you. Kick the habit now!

— — You'd rather collect food stamps than work at the health-food store.

—— You would kill the goose that laid the golden egg for a spoonful of *foie gras*.

28.
PREPONDERANCE OF THE GREAT

Things are fast reaching the breaking point.
Revolution is not required, but you better start creating a transition strategy.

— — You're in over your head. You'll probably drown. But you still did the right thing.

—— The situation's as if your grandmother remarried. Nice wedding, but no chance of children.

—— A hero appears to save the day. But if he's a self-serving prima donna. The day wasn't worth saving.

—— You bull-headed idiot! You won't listen to anyone. You're going full steam ahead into disaster.

—— Old grass-roots support can create an entirely new movement.

— — Before you start building your enterprise, put some padding on the floor.

Don't give up.

29.
THE ABYSMAL (WATER)

Double danger. So much danger you're actually starting to think straight again. Scary isn't it?
You can only do what must be done to survive. Your example will teach others.

You blew every chance to get out of this mess. You'll be tied up for a long time.
There's a chance to save your bacon. Do that now. Save the world later.
Even in the middle of a dangerous situation, stay sincere and humble.
Things are hairy in front of you and in back of you. Still . . . don't move.
It's too soon to get out of danger. But you can do some small things that will help.
You're getting so used to danger it's part of you. You grow crazy and self-destructive.

30.
THE CLINGING, FIRE

Success. Be as mellow and docile as a happy cow.
Keep that attitude and your light will shine everywhere.

Kill the generals! Spare the soldiers! Destroy bad habits! Keep the ones that aren't so bad.
Don't cling to either hope or fear. After all, in the long run, what good does it do?
It's a shooting star! It lights the sky, but for only an instant. Will you be a burnout too?
It's sunset! Time to party till you puke, or complain about how short life is. Both get you nowhere.
It's noon! The Sun shines bright yellow. Balance, harmony, and beauty (and lunch).
It's morning! Your mind's going a million miles an hour. Focus and get going.

For everything there is a season.

31.
INFLUENCE (WOOING)

Mutual attraction. Courtship, not seduction.
The man's on his knees, but the woman's in control.
Be happy to give people your advice, but don't act like a know-it-all.

-- -- Lots of talk. Nothing said. Empty words. Empty head.

—— Your will remains firm. No need to guilt-trip yourself.

—— You're following your heart. Many are impressed, but you'll blow it if you try to manipulate them.

—— Don't go off half-cocked trying to woo the whole world, when only a select few will respond.

-- -- No need to move until you have somewhere to go.

-- -- You won't walk very far by just wiggling your toes.

32.
DURATION

Marriage. The courtship's over. The man gets off his knees. (The woman's still in control.)
Living force and energy—enduring because it is flexible—moving yet stable, like the stars.

-- -- Hurry, hurry, hurry. Go, go, go. Die, die, die.

-- -- Old traditions may seem safe and comfortable, but you'll turn to stone if you don't stay flexible.

—— What you're looking for may not be in the place you're looking.

—— Wallowing in fear and doubt attracts fear and doubt. Stop it before you embarrass yourself.

—— Don't worry if you're overqualified for this little chore. It'll be fun. You'll do great.

-- -- Oh! You're too impatient. These things take time.

Like a trodden serpent, turn and strike!

33.
RETREAT

**Perfect time to retreat—now, while it's not a life-and-death struggle and you still
have some power and influence.**
Little acts of resistance will keep the enemy from advancing too far.

—— Retreating at this moment is the correct thing to do. Don't give it another thought.
—— Retreating at the perfect moment is not unpleasant. Don't sweat the small stuff.
—— Make up your mind and happily retreat. It just kills your enemy when you do that.
—— There comes a time when you have to "hire" the very people who could imprison you.
— — Even jerks are saved if their hearts are in the right place and they don't let go of the
hero's skirt.
— — You're at the tail end of a retreating army. For god's sake, don't moon the guys chasing you.

34.
THE POWER OF THE GREAT

Goodness and truth have come to power. Direct that power wisely.
The established order is currently great and just. Don't move against it.

— — Can't go back or move forward. Try, and it gets worse. Do nothing. Eventually you'll get
going.
— — It's a cakewalk from here on. Stop acting so macho and be a good winner.
—— Subtle power comes from within. It removes resistance without creating more resistance.
—— President for four days and he sends the army overseas. Four years later . . . they're still
there.
—— Success is coming, and it's well deserved. Things look so good you may get cocky. Don't!
—— At the moment, you'll only break your foot if you try to kick down the door.

35.
PROGRESS

Progress. Promotion. Honor (a raise?).
You're a bright boy (girl). Your boss is hip and pulls you up the corporate ladder.

—— A little terror is sometimes helpful in motivating your employees. But don't get carried away.

—— Win some—lose some. Don't sweat it if you're making the world a little better.

—— In times like these, even dishonest jerks can get rich. You stay clean. They'll get busted.

—— The team is backing your plan. Things are moving forward. So what if you lost a little control?

—— Oh no! The boss's secretary won't let you in to see him. Don't panic. You're still his boy (girl).

—— You ran your idea up the flagpole. Nobody saluted. Don't sweat it. They'll come around.

36.
DARKENING OF THE LIGHT

Goodness is wounded. The bad guy's got a gun and he's hunting good guys.
Don't panic. Maintain a low profile. Don't snuff your light; just hide it for a while.

—— Headline: "Darkness Overcomes Light—then Commits Suicide."

—— You're stuck as a soldier in the bad guy's army. Stay true to yourself and keep your head down.

—— You're close to the bad-guy leader. You learn his evil plan. Get out before the poop starts flying.

—— Good guy accidentally seizes bad-guy leader. Great! But don't try to repair all his damage at once.

—— It's only a flesh wound. Forget about it and get busy saving the others.

—— Unable to rise above this mess, you're scrambling. Friends don't understand and start to gossip.

Maybe you already are on the top of the heap.

37.
The Family (The Clan)

The functional family models the functional society. The dysfunctional family models the dysfunctional society.

Back up your words with the proper example. "Do as I say," must really mean "Do as I do."

— Dad stays in charge of us because he stays in charge of himself.

— Dad is so cool. He doesn't try to terrorize us. We follow his orders because we know he loves us.

— — Moms and good CFOs really know how to keep the organization well fed and profitable.

— "Spare the rod, spoil the child." That's ridiculous! However, when in doubt . . . go for the rod.

— — Stay focused on the duties right under your nose.

— Getting spoiled before learning your place is a bummer for everyone.

Some days, it doesn't pay to get out of bed.

38.
Opposition

There's still too much disagreement to get anything really important done. Little things? Maybe.

You can party with surfers, but keep your shirt and tie on.

— This devil you're fighting is actually your best friend. Drop your gun and give him a hug.

— — How can this bum possibly help you? Look harder, you idiot. He'll save your sorry hide!

— Everyone is against you. No! There's one who's just like you. Success if you link up.

— — It's horrible. How can you possibly overcome all this opposition? You can—and you will.

— Can't agree at work? Maybe you two should bump into each other at a bar.

— Opposition within the team? Sit tight. Cool guys come back on their own. Jerks self-destruct.

39.
Obstruction

You can't climb over this problem. You're going to have to go around it. Blaming others won't work. By fixing the problem inside yourself, you'll fix the problem outside yourself.

-- -- Headline: "Old General Comes out of Retirement to Kick some Butts."

—— This is an emergency. You have to pitch in. Wow! And look! Friends are coming to help.

-- -- Sure, you can lead the charge, but will anyone follow? Wait and muster some troops. Then charge.

—— Screw this battle! You've got a wife and kids to feed. Go back home.

-- -- Even if it means making things worse, your duty dictates that you tackle this head-on.

-- -- Back off and look for the best moment to act.

40.
Deliverance

Be a gracious winner and return to normalcy as soon as possible. Forgive mistakes and misplaced loyalties, but immediately execute the last few hardcore troublemakers.

-- -- Now is the correct time to put the good-for-nothing tyrant against the wall and shoot him.

-- -- Don't hang out with people you'd rather see leave town.

—— To gain influence to do great things, you're going to have to dump your old drinking buddies.

-- -- Not knowing how to be cool (like real aristocrats), newly rich idiots attract ridicule and robbers.

—— The struggle has rewarded you with strength of character.

-- -- Well-deserved R & R after the battle's won. Quiet. Peaceful.

She loves you not.

41.
DECREASE

A downturn in the economy—less stuff, less time, less energy.
Don't get mad. Become simpler. Make it an art form.

—— It's possible to become wealthy without making someone else poor. Be a philanthropist.
— — You lucky devil! Your good fortune has been ordained by the gods.
— — By decreasing your bad habits and flaws, you increase your friends and supporters.
— — Three's a crowd. One's a magnet. Two's good company.
—— Give up your time. Give up your resources. But don't give up your dignity and your soul.
—— It's fine to be a charity volunteer, but don't neglect your own family's needs.

42.
INCREASE

An upturn in the economy—more stuff, more time, more energy.
It won't last forever, so do great things while you can. Start by imitating great deeds.

—— He who is filthy rich yet withholds his wealth from the needy is not rich—just filthy. Beat him up.
—— No need to even think about recognition. Kindness is its own reward—its own recognition.
— — A good middle manager makes sure the wealth gets spread around.
— — Times are so good even horrible events and accidents bring riches and good luck.
— — Love and goodwill are now so strong that not even your bad horoscope can stop this flood of increase.
—— Somebody has the money, but not the energy. You've got the energy. A perfect marriage!

43.
Breakthrough (Resoluteness)

Compromise with jerks is not an option. But what will you gain if you become a jerk to battle them?
Expose them and brand them. But first expose and brand the jerk in you.

— — Victory? Don't celebrate until all pockets of evil have been rooted out. Otherwise you're dead.

——— Weeds will continue to come back. Continue to pull them up.

——— You are inwardly stubborn and it just kills you that you can't advance. Can you just let it go? It's doubtful.

——— You've a lowly friend in the enemy camp. Nobody understands. They call you a traitor. It's OK.

——— Be vigilant. Be prepared. Be armed. When the attack comes, you won't freak out.

——— Don't stick your neck out too far at first. Unexpected problems often crop up at the beginning.

44.
Coming to Meet

You mistakenly thought that hooker was too weak to cause trouble, so you gave her your home number.
Even if you're far from home, don't let 'em forget who's boss. Start giving orders.

——— You may be above it all. If so, don't be so irritated by all the idiots beneath you.

——— There's no need to micromanage the troops. Even the idiots will rise to the occasion.

——— Now's no time to be a snob. You're going to need those "little people." Be nice to them.

——— You're thinking about being naughty. Snap out of it!

——— Control this situation with a gentle hand—but control it. Don't let it infect other areas of your life.

— — Get mad! Stop this nonsense *now!* If it comes back—stop it again!

Do what it takes to sleep better.

45.
Gathering Together (Massing)

The moment has arrived for a mass movement.
If it forms around an extraordinary individual, great things will be done.

—— —— A potential ally misunderstands your motives. Damn! Don't panic. He or she will soon see the light.

———— By staying strong and true to yourself, you transform groupies into real supporters.

———— You've delivered the votes for your candidate. Good for you. Success.

—— —— So what if you're the odd man out? Don't be shy. Get on board.

—— —— This thing's bigger than all of us. We've come together for a reason.

—— —— Stop vacillating! You won't be sorry you supported this guy. Offer your hand. He'll grab it.

Don't just stand on the porch. Knock on the door.

46.
Pushing Upward

Onward and upward! Focus your will and act. Be flexible, but keep pushing.
Consult with the highest authorities. They're ready to listen to you.

—— —— Blindly pushing—wasting energy—lousy idea!

—— —— Continuing successes. So far, so good. Stay sober and keep it up.

—— —— You've pushed up to the top. The goal is gloriously achieved!

———— Pure unobstructed progress and growth. Don't be distracted by thoughts that it may not last forever.

———— This guy's (gal's) an oddball. But you know I think he's (she's) going all the way to the top.

—— —— All systems are "Go." Now! A perfect liftoff.

47.
OPPRESSION (EXHAUSTION)

Sorry! Out of steam. Out of luck. No matter how much you whine or argue, nobody's going to listen.
If you can stay cheerful through this terrible period, the cheerfulness will be the key to your salvation.

I know. It's been bad and now you're spooked. Go ahead now. You won't regret it.

No help from the folks who need you. No help from the folks you need. Wait it out . . . and pray!

You'd like to help the needy, but hesitate because of your snobby friends. Screw them. Just do it!

Bummed out about the wrong things, you turn to stupid things for support.
Your spouse leaves you.

If you can't stop sulking, you'll miss approaching opportunities.

If you surrender to depression, you'll stay depressed a long time. You have to snap out of it.

48.
THE WELL

Our positions in life may differ, but we're all basically the same. We all draw water from the same well.
If you break your bucket or your rope's too short, you're out of luck, buddy.

Happy days are here again. Drinks are on the house—the good stuff! Is everybody happy? Yes!

Wisdom, like pure water, is no good unless you drink of it. Potential's just potential until you act.

You help no one but yourself while you pull your act together. Afterward, you help everybody.

Someone who is absolutely perfect for this job is being overlooked.
Wake up the decision-maker!

Not only is opportunity being overlooked, you couldn't take advantage of it if you saw it.

Yuk! Muddy water. This person or situation is completely rotten—no good for anything anymore.

Look around.
Your question has
already been answered.

49.
REVOLUTION (MOLTING)

Revolution! Can you lead the mob without causing a reign of terror or becoming a worse tyrant yourself?
Take note of the cycles. You can organize this chaos.

── ──   After the revolution, stability—and a bunch of tiny hassles and a bunch of whining idiots.

──────   Don't even ask the oracle. It's obvious who is going to lead this revolution.

──────   If you're truly guided by inner truth, then it's time for a total and radical change of government.

──────   Don't be hasty or too vicious. Change only those things that everybody grumbles about a lot!

── ──   Done everything to prevent this? Got a worthy goal? Good plan? Good leader? OK! *Revolt!*

──────   Your back's not completely against the wall yet. It's too soon to revolt! You'd get creamed.

50.
THE CALDRON

Extremely good luck is being served up. Culture blossoms. Civilization advances. Prophets are honored.
Discovering your will is the wood. Doing your will is the fire. Enjoy the warmth and light. There is no law beyond "Do what thou wilt."

──────   Supreme good luck. Somebody's being so good that even the gods notice.

── ──   Stay self-effacing and humble. It's the best way to keep smart and loyal supporters.

──────   Headline: "Unworthy President Gets Drunk—Pukes on Japanese President."

──────   I know. Your talents are being wasted because nobody recognizes you. That will change.

──────   Hell yes, they're jealous of your success (with good reason). Don't rub it in. Things will be cool.

── ──   Refuse none. Everyone, regardless of station, can rise to the occasion and be recognized.

51.
THE AROUSING (SHOCK, THUNDER)

Boo! Scared you, didn't it? It scared everyone else too! Ha ha. That's only natural. When you've got your poop together, you should never really be afraid.

-- -- Blitzkrieg! Neighbors are blown to smithereens. If you can walk, you may get to safety.

-- -- Bam! Bam! Bam! Nonstop shocks. It's irritating, but you really don't get hurt.

—— Stuck in the mud. Nothing to fight. Nowhere to go.

-- -- Wow! That was a wakeup call! Change your ways and don't be caught snoozing again.

-- -- A shocking loss. It's terrible. There's nothing to do now but write it off. (You'll get it back.)

—— Oh! Man! That nearly scared me to death. Ha ha. Thought you had me there, didn't you?

52.
KEEPING STILL, MAINTAIN

Find a quiet place away from people and noises. Forget your body for a while. Go inside and meet yourself.
Keep focused on the present situation. Thinking beyond that will only bum you out and waste your time.

—— You have achieved supreme hipness—calm, cool, and serene.

-- -- For god's sake, keep your mouth shut or you'll get yourself in deep doo-doo.

-- -- Can't quite get rid of the ego, eh? Hang in there. You can't throw the ego away. It must be lost.

—— You're being forced to shut up. You're smoldering. Calmness needs to come naturally.

-- -- Your leader is sweeping you and the troops straight to hell. You're not strong enough to stop it.

-- -- Stop before you start. No action—no chance for mistakes. The time for action soon appears.

They can do that to you.

53.
DEVELOPMENT (GRADUAL PROGRESS)

Slow but sure. No need to be hasty. Be patient. Proceed gradually, one step at a time. Progress remains stable and strong by growing slowly.

—— Well done. Your life's work is completed. Your biography will inspire the world.

—— You're screwed! Coworkers poison the boss's mind against you. Slowly this will improve.

— — You're a lamb at a party full of wolves. Find a dark spot near the door and maintain a low profile.

—— You idiot! Couldn't wait, could you? Now you'll have to fight like hell if you expect to make it.

— — Your first promotion. You're feeling a little more sure of yourself. Treat the gang to dinner.

— — Hey rookie! Nobody helps you. Everybody picks on you. Take it slow and easy. You'll make it.

54.
THE MARRYING MAIDEN

Watch your step. You're pretty damned low on this totem pole. You won't be able to force anything.
Bite the bullet and keep your eye on the prize.

— — Empty forms. Empty gestures. This is going nowhere. Nothing will help.

— — So what if this guy's not a blue blood. Don't be a snob. He'll transform you into a very happy wife.

—— Rather than be a slut, you risk becoming an old maid. Finally, you meet a guy who digs virtuous old gals.

— — Oh! You're such a little slut!

—— Carry on even if you are abandoned.

—— Your boss confides in you, even though your job is funky. Behind the scenes you can help.

You may have to be the grown-up.

55.
ABUNDANCE (FULLNESS)

You've hit the jackpot! This is the answer you were hoping to receive. Enjoy it while it lasts.

Your mind and vision are clear. The punishments you dole out will be just.

- ▬ ▬ In gaining everything you want, you've become an arrogant, selfish, lonely old fool.
- ▬ ▬ It's all coming together. You're getting good advice. Fame, fortune, and good luck are coming.
- ▬▬▬ Things are starting to clear up. Allies join and put their heads together.
- ▬▬▬ Idiots are monopolizing the action. Your hands are tied. Don't beat yourself up. It's not your fault.
- ▬ ▬ There's been a coup and the new guys are real stinkers. Don't try to be a hero. Stay cool and wait.
- ▬▬▬ Your star is so bright you can powwow with the bigwigs and really get stuff done.

56.
THE WANDERER

Howdy stranger. Just passin' through? Stay friendly and don't cause no trouble. Ya hear?

Short fair trials and swift fair punishment. That's our motto.

- ▬▬▬ The stranger has had too much fun and forgotten to be discreet. Big trouble. He loses everything.
- ▬ ▬ Your new job takes you far from home. That's good! You've got great letters of recommendation.
- ▬▬▬ It's a drag being a stranger. You've a place to crash and a few things, but you're not happy or safe.
- ▬▬▬ I trusted you, stranger. You insult my family, bust up my house, drink all my liquor. Now get out!
- ▬ ▬ Welcome, stranger. I like your style. I trust you. Stay at my place. Need a job while in town?
- ▬ ▬ Humility becomes a stranger. But keep your dignity. Don't encourage idiots to humiliate you.

The only truly good karma is no karma.

57.
THE GENTLE (THE PENETRATING WIND)

Success through small, subtle, but persistent means.
Don't freak people out by acting unexpectedly. Gently prepare them for what's coming.

——— You've found your secret enemies, but you're too weak to fight them. Lay low and lurk.

——— Think hard before you act here. Then watch carefully to make sure it was the wise thing to do.

—— —— All right! You bring home the bacon, not only for your family, but also for guests and the gods.

——— You're in danger of overthinking this thing. Act or face humiliation.

——— Secret enemies plot your doom. Hire priests to identify them and—wizards to destroy them.

—— —— Like a soldier, firmly decide when to advance or firmly decide when to retreat.

58.
THE JOYOUS, LAKE

Joy springs from deep happiness. Be friendly and cheerful. It's contagious.
Enjoy gatherings with happy and intelligent friends. Have fun and learn from one another.

—— —— Seduced by the dark side, you're no longer your own man (woman).

——— You're not above making a mistake or two. Play with fire and you get burned. Wear gloves.

——— Make up your mind—which will it be? Passionate dissipation or true inner joy?

—— —— Wild and crazy diversions. Emptiness attracts emptiness.

——— There's no real joy in indulging in low pleasures.

——— You free yourself by possessing joy within.

Now go out there and be a star!

59.
DISPERSION (DISSOLUTION)

Solve et Coagula. **It's the ego that needs dissolving here. Then things can be brought back together.**
Religion and spiritual practices can do both.

—— You save your family and friends from danger.

—— A great idea saves the day!

— — It takes a real visionary to see the big picture. You may have to dissolve some pretty weird stuff.

— — The mission is so important that you must dissolve all feelings of self-interest.

—— Bummed out? Depressed? Dissolve that ill humor before it dissolves you.

— — Dissolve misunderstandings at the very beginning. Strangle them at birth!

60.
LIMITATION

It's good to be frugal. It's good to be temperate. But don't get carried away. Limit your limits also.
Limits set by duty—limits set voluntarily. Limits hold us together.

— — People hate totalitarian restrictions. But sometimes you need to be a real fascist with yourself.

—— Look how much you've done with so little. Everyone's really impressed.

— — Wow! This limitation has made things easier.

— — Oh, my head! When will I ever learn to say, "Enough is enough! I'm going home now."

—— Now's no time to stay home and dawdle. You have to get out and act now!

—— It's time to be discreet and stay close to home.

It's only money.

61.
INNER TRUTH

The purity and strength of the truth inside you inspires all—even good-for-nothing jerks and morons.
Flush your prejudices down the toilet and put yourself for a moment in the other guy's shoes.

—— Phony charisma! All flash and no heat. All clucking and no eggs.
—— Wow! You have the charisma that will hold this thing together.
— — Listen to the source of your inner truth. Resist distractions. Keep your eye on the ball.
— — You depend on other people to make you happy. Bad mistake. Only you can make yourself happy.
—— If the song is from your heart, first your friends will applaud, then your city, then the whole world.
—— A secret relationship robs you of your inner freedom. This is really going to screw you up.

Take a deep breath and ask again.

62.
PREPONDERANCE OF THE SMALL

Keep your expectations low. Don't expect big things to come out of this. Concentrate on the little stuff.
Keep it simple and unpretentious. Do the correct thing, in the correct way, at the correct time.

— — You've bitten off more than you can chew. Still you try to swallow it. You're dead meat!
— — Remember the seven samurai? Great warriors out of work. You need those guys right now.
—— It's going to be difficult, but you must stay cool and resist all temptation to do anything here.
—— Sure, you're cool. But don't be so sure of yourself that you forget to watch your back.
— — Your boss makes an appointment with you. He stands you up. Don't throw a fit. Go back to work.
— — Don't try to run before you can walk. You'll end up breaking your leg, your furniture, and your heart.

63.

AFTER COMPLETION

The new order begins. It's so balanced and perfect. You're tempted to just relax and enjoy. Big mistake.

Are you wise enough to spot the potential for decay and trouble in all this blissful perfection?

—— Don't stop and brag about the dangers you've overcome. You're only halfway through the woods.

—— The widow's mite is more pleasing to the gods than the rich man's gold pieces.

—— What's this? Embarrassing scandal. It can still be covered up. See that it doesn't happen again.

—— The new order is in place. Now begins the long struggle to expand. Don't colonize with bums.

—— Not getting the attention you deserve? Don't pursue it. And certainly don't play the clown to get it.

—— Leave the celebration early. You may get off with just a slight hangover. Others . . . not so lucky.

Don't invade Russia with winter coming on.

64.

BEFORE COMPLETION

Things are difficult, but there is great promise. Be careful and very deliberate. You could still blow it.

Do your due diligence before proceeding.

—— Victory is assured. Drink with your allies and loved ones. Get mellow (but not drunk).

—— Victory, sweet victory! Everything works out. A fresh new world begins.

—— It's time to fight like the devil. Don't wimp out now. When the smoke clears, you'll be on top!

—— The time is right, but you don't have the power to facilitate the change. Create another situation.

—— Don't drive off yet, but start the car and warm 'er up.

—— Move now and this will blow up in your face. Save yourself some embarrassment. Don't start.

TABLE 12. SIXTY-FOUR I CHING HEXAGRAMS

	☰	☳	☵	☶	☷	☴	☲	☱
☰	1	34	5	26	11	9	14	43
☳	25	51	3	27	24	42	21	17
☵	6	40	29	4	7	59	64	47
☶	33	62	39	52	15	53	56	31
☷	12	16	8	23	2	20	35	45
☴	44	32	48	18	46	57	50	28
☲	13	55	63	22	36	37	30	49
☱	10	54	60	41	19	61	38	58

NOTES

Chapter 2

1 Stephen Hawking, *A Brief History of Time* (New York: Bantam Books, 1988), p. 152.

2 Israel Regardie, *The Complete Golden Dawn System of Magick* (Tempe, AZ: New Falcon Publications, 2003), p. 25.

Chapter 5

1 Stephen Hawking, *Black Holes and Baby Universes and Other Essay* (New York: Bantam Books, 1993), p. 70.

2 The *Mahabharata* and the *Ramayama* are two most important epic Hindu scriptures. The familiar *Bhagavad Gita* is just a tiny portion of the *Mahabharata*.

3 In the 8th century B.C., the Egyptian calendar was extended from 360 to 365 days to synchronize the traditional lunar calendar with the solar year marked by the rising of Sirius and the inundation of the Nile.

Chapter 7

1 Margarete Ward, *Gong Hee Fot Choy (Greeting of Riches),* 54th ed. (Berkley, CA: Celestial Arts 1997).

Chapter 12

1 Greg Nielsen and Joseph Polansky, *Pendulum Power* (Rochester VT: Destiny Books, 1987), p. 7.

2 Puck, the playful spirit prankster of Shakespeare's *Midsummer's Night Dream* took his name from Pooka.

I don't know. Use the pendulum and a book.

Chapter 13

1 John Blofeld, *I Ching (The Book of Changes): A New Translation of the Ancient Chinese Text with Detailed Instructions for Its Practical Use in Divination* (New York: Dutton and Co., Inc. 1968), p. 85.

2 Copyright 1950 by Bollingen Foundation Inc. Reprinted with corrections by Princeton University Press (Princeton, NJ: Princeton University Press, 3rd edition, 1969).

3. John Blofeld, *I Ching (The Book of Changes)*.

Show a little backbone!

ABOUT THE AUTHOR

Best-selling author Rachael Pollack calls Lon Milo DuQuette "that rarest of writers: a man who knows his subject from the inside out and at the same time can write clearly and gracefully."

Author of a dozen books (translated into five languages) on tarot, magick, and the occult, DuQuette is praised by critics as "*the most entertaining author in the field today.*" His lectures around the world have been described as a delightful combination of wisdom, laughter, and soul-searching terror. A second generation native Californian, he and his wife, Constance, live in Costa Mesa, California.

take it
slow and steady.

An old friend
gives good advice.

Feast! rejoice!
there is no dread
hereafter!

You've fought
the good fight.

Be kind
to your pets.

Show some
class and let this matter
drop.